# SHAUN RYDER

## How to be a Rock Star

**Shaun Ryder**, the lead singer of Happy Mondays and Black Grape, was the Keith Richards *and* Mick Jagger of his generation. A true rebel, who formed and led not one but two seminal bands, he's had number-one albums, headlined Glastonbury, toured the world numerous times, taken every drug under the sun, been through rehab – and come out the other side as a national treasure.

*'Show me a boy who never wanted to be a rock star and I'll show you a liar'*

# SHAUN RYDER
## How to be a Rock Star

With Luke Bainbridge

ALLEN&UNWIN

Published in hardback and trade paperback in Great Britain in 2021 by
Allen & Unwin, an imprint of Atlantic Books Ltd.

This paperback edition published in Great Britain in 2022 by
Allen & Unwin, an imprint of Atlantic Books Ltd.

10 9 8 7 6 5 4 3 2 1

A CIP catalogue record for this book is available from the British Library.

Paperback ISBN: 978 1 83895 327 0
E-book ISBN: 978 1 83895 326 3

Printed in Great Britain by Clays Ltd, Elcograf S.p.A.

Allen & Unwin
An imprint of Atlantic Books Ltd
Ormond House
26–27 Boswell Street
London
WC1N 3JZ

www.allenandunwin.com/uk

*For my wife and children*

*With thanks to Alan McGee, Anita Heryet,
and all my crew*

# Contents

# Intro

As far back as I can remember, I always wanted to be a rock star. It's the first thing I ever *really* wanted to be. Probably the *only* thing I've ever wanted to be. I never really wanted to be an astronaut or a footballer, or any of those things that other young kids wanted to be. I wanted to be a rock star.

I can remember watching Bowie on *Top of the Pops* and the Small Faces and thinking how cool they looked and asking my mam if I could get my hair cut like Steve Marriott. But it was when I saw the films *That'll Be The Day* and *Stardust* that the idea really took hold in my head. I used to bunk off school and sneak into the cinema in the afternoon. Those films came out in 1973 and 1974, so I would have been about twelve at the time. That was when I first got the idea of what it was like to be a rock star. David Essex starred in both films. In *That'll Be The Day*, he was doing odd jobs and thinking about getting in a band. Then in *Stardust*, his band actually made it and he became a rock star. The great thing about both films was they were about more than the music; they were about the whole lifestyle and fashion that came with the music. When his manager, who was played by Adam Faith, said: 'I supply the birds, the pills and the pot,' I was sat there in the cinema, bunking off school, and I thought, 'I want a bit of that!'

I had no idea how I might go about it. I couldn't play an instrument or read music, so it was a complete pipedream really, but it was one thing I could see myself doing. It was the lifestyle as much as the music. I can't really remember wanting to be anything else. Although I'm sure I'm not unique in that. I'm sure every kid in the cinema was thinking the same as me. It was just like the tagline in *Stardust* says: 'Show me a boy who never wanted to be a rock star and I'll show you a liar.'

I could also relate quite a bit to the David Essex character in the film, and he weirdly mirrored how my life panned out a bit. He left school without qualifications like me, nearly got settled down early like me, and then was in a job that wasn't really going anywhere (he worked on the dodgems on a fair, and I was a postman), before he started a band and they eventually took off. I wasn't even put off when he died of an overdose at the end. I mean, obviously I didn't want to die of an overdose, but the possibility of that happening didn't overshadow the attraction of becoming a rock star. I was sold. I was in.

I had no idea how I was going to do it. I loved music but couldn't play an instrument. But I got more and more determined as time when on. I left school at fourteen and went to work as a post boy for the Post Office and that brought it home to me that I needed to find a way out. I didn't want to wake up in forty years' time and still be doing a post round. No disrespect to postmen, but I thought there was a bit more out there. Another way. There were only a couple of ways out for a kid like me from Salford back then: to make it as a footballer or maybe a boxer. Hopefully there's a few more opportunities for kids from Salford nowadays, but that's the way it was back then. Those were your routes out. I began to realize that being a rock star could be a way out too.

We were rock stars before we even had a band, in our little way. I'd always been known around our way when I was growing up. I was a bit notorious, I suppose you could say, and my reputation preceded me a bit. Same with Bez. We were both living rock'n'roll lives before we met. The sex and the drugs came before the rock'n'roll really.

The truth is there's no fail-safe guide to being a rock star. I'll tell you as much about my experience in this book as I can, and about what it was like for me, and hopefully some of it will be useful or at least entertaining. But I'll let you in on a secret: most rock stars are making it up as they go along. It's not something you can be taught really. I know there's some Svengalis who think they can mastermind bands like they're a puppeteer, but those are pop bands really, from The Monkees to Take That. Maybe you can teach someone to be a pop star, but I don't think you can teach someone to be a rock star.

There are some rock stars who stride out on stage in front of 70,000 people, thinking 'THIS is where I belong, I was

BORN to do this. I deserve to have 70,000 people staring at me, cheering my every word,' but there's not many like that, and I'm certainly not one of them. I think most musicians and rock stars suffer from self-doubt at one stage or another. Half the time when some rock star is giving it out about being the greatest in the world, that's just bravado covering up for their self-doubt. Or maybe it's the drugs talking.

But if you're going to last any distance in this game, then you have to find a way of becoming comfortable with that. You have to find a way of having a bit of an ego without being a dick and without worrying too much about it. None of it is real, and it's important to remember that. The music is important, and you can't last without good tunes, but a lot of the rest of it is smoke and mirrors. That's why I find bigger gigs easier to do, which may surprise some people, but they're easier because they just seem surreal and the huge audience is just a mass of people, so it's easier to get in the mindset of playing the rock star. The hardest gigs are the little intimate ones. It's hard to be a rock star and swivelling your hips when you can see the whites of everyone's eyes staring at you.

The other thing I would say is that it's bloody hard work. It's a slog to get started, and to get noticed, and touring never becomes that easy. You're away from the family and there are times when everyone wants a piece of you and you feel like you're getting hassled all the time. But having been a postman for a few years when I was younger, I know the alternative is much more of a slog, so I'm never not grateful. There's nothing more annoying than a rock star banging on about how hard their life is.

I never wanted to be like anyone else. I never wanted to be Mick Jagger or David Bowie or Ian Curtis. I wanted to be Shaun Ryder, but Shaun Ryder as a rock star! Of course there were bands that me and the rest of the bands were really into, but we never wanted to copy anyone else or sound like anyone else. In the very early rehearsals we used to do a few cover versions – Joy Division mainly – but that was just us learning our instruments, not because we wanted to sound like Joy Division. Why would you want to do that? I never understood that. When we first started trying to write our own songs, if Mark Day, our guitarist, or our kid on bass came up with something that sounded like someone else – even if it was a band we were really into like The Beatles or Joy Division – we'd go, 'Nah, get rid of that, sounds too much like The Beatles,' or 'Sack that, it reminds me of Joy Division.' We were all on the same page: we wanted to create our own sound that was different to everyone else. We didn't realize how unusual that was at the time. Most bands who are starting out and first trying to make a noise and write songs would love it if they came up with something that sounded like one of their heroes, but we were the opposite. Which is why we developed our own sound that didn't sound like anything else, and that's what first got us noticed. Mike Pickering, who was a DJ at the Haçienda, produced one of our first singles and went on to form M People, said that Andrew Berry (the lead singer of The Weeds, who we did some early gigs with) told him that he thought we sounded 'pure'. He said we sounded like we didn't have any previous influences, as though we had been locked in a time capsule and not affected by anything that was around in current popular culture. That's exactly what I wanted.

As soon as we started, I wanted us to be big. I wanted to be on *Top of the Pops*. I didn't want to be a cult band who was playing to 150 people every night. I wanted to be playing huge gigs and going round the world. If you're going to do it, do it right. I saw rock'n'roll as my ticket out of there, and I was determined to do whatever it took to make it happen. I realized pretty quickly that you needed to play the game a little bit, everybody does. Look at all the biggest bands in the world – from The Beatles and The Stones to U2 and Coldplay – and they've all played the game a bit, certainly in the early days when they were trying to make it. I don't mean music-wise. Don't go changing your sound to try and jump on the bandwagon of whatever is cool at the time, just to get noticed, that's the last thing you should do. If you try and follow whatever music is fashionable at the time, then you'll get left behind when the next thing comes along. There's that saying about fashion: 'Don't be a peacock, because you'll be a feather duster tomorrow.' Same is true with music. When I say 'play the game', I mean all the nonsense that goes with it. All the press and the promo, the photoshoots and the videos and the TV appearances and all that stuff. Some bands make the mistake of thinking they're too cool to promote their own music. I never understood that, not promoting your own music. I was never too precious about not doing this or that, because it wasn't cool. Not doing an interview with that magazine or newspaper because they weren't perceived to be cool? Fuck that. I wanted the band to get as much exposure as possible. There's nothing less 'cool' than dickheads trying too hard be cool. Most of those bands from back then who would only speak to the music press and were pretentious about doing anything that wasn't 'cool' have been completely forgotten about. Trust me, if you're only considered a 'cool' band, that 'cool' crowd will quickly move on to the next thing, and before you know it you're yesterday's news.

I knew that was the way we could try and make our band last, to get some longevity, by getting people talking about us. I think a lot of people think that me and the Mondays were so busy partying and living that rock'n'roll life, like an outlaw gang, that we didn't give a fuck if we crashed and burned. Not me. No way. We had come from nothing and, even though we were determined to enjoy the rock'n'roll behaviour and party harder than anyone else, I wanted to make sure it lasted.

That said, I never dreamed we would last as long as we have. Happy Mondays have been going for nearly forty years now and The Beatles only lasted ten years, so the Mondays have been going four times as long as The Beatles! (Although we did fall out and have a couple of breaks in transmission along the way, but we'll get to that later.) When we made our first album in 1986, it had been eighteen years since *Sgt Pepper's* but that felt like ancient history as far as we were concerned – like something that happened in our mam and dad's generation. Now our debut album is thirty-six years old: twice as old as *Sgt Pepper's* was then!

It's great that young kids are into us now, when we've been going nearly forty years. That's like me as a teenager, in the seventies, being into someone who had started out in the 1930s! Me as a teenager, being bang into some big swing band like the Glenn Miller Band or something. Which is a bit mad when you think of it like that. But it's great. People forget that if rock'n'roll was born in the fifties with Little Richard and Elvis, then it's still only about seventy years old now, and the Mondays arrived halfway through that.

I wanted the Mondays to be original and I wanted them to be huge. What's the point otherwise? As far as I'm concerned, if you're making music, you want as many people as possible to hear it. That's what it was about for me, not being worshipped as a rock god. I never saw myself like that. I was never one for making grand claims about the Mondays being the saviours of rock'n'roll or anything. I was happy to leave that to the Stone Roses or Oasis, who were always coming out with grandiose statements like that. Oasis came along after us and when they did *Top of the Pops* for 'Live Forever' Noel said, 'It's all about ambition… we want to be an important band. Making music for a closet full of people in Bradford doesn't mean anything. Phil Collins has to be chased out of the charts, Wet Wet Wet and all that. The only way is to get in there amongst them, stamp the fuckers out.' The Mondays were really ambitious as well. I just didn't shout it from the rooftops like they did. But it was also about making a future for ourselves.

I've been lucky that people have always been interested in what Shaun Ryder is going to do next, even if it's something unusual like ghost hunting, chasing UFOs, doing a duet with an opera singer like Russell Watson, trying to be a stand-up comedian for Stand Up To Cancer, or living with a tribe in the Amazonian jungle. I always get loads of mad offers, and as I get older I enjoy doing more mainstream TV and stuff that I probably would have turned down twenty years ago. It's important as well, if we want to reach a new audience for the music. We represent a moment in time for a lot of people and we were the soundtrack to their formative years. We remind them of the halcyon days of their youth, which is great. But that's not enough really, for a band to keep going. Those people are in their forties and fifties now and some of them still go out to gigs and festivals, but a lot don't, so as a band you need to bring in the younger generation as well, and that's where reality TV comes in. I'm more of an all-round entertainer now. I'm family-friendly. Or a lot more family-friendly than I used to be! Back in the nineties I was the first person to be banned from live TV by Channel 4 because of my bad language.

I do a lot more TV work now, especially after I went into the jungle for *I'm A Celebrity… Get Me Out Of Here!* I've always been asked to do all sorts of reality shows, but turned them all down because I never watched them at home and didn't really see the appeal. Until Bez did *Big Brother*, then I realized just how big reality TV had become. When Bez came out of the *Big Brother* house he was the most famous man in Manchester and was getting offered all sorts. Funnily enough, it was actually me who first got the offer from *Big Brother*. They wanted me to go in the house but I wasn't up for it, not least because I was still in a battle with my dickhead ex-managers, so any money I earned went straight to them. So I told *Big Brother* to get Bez in instead, and he only went and won it. Nowadays I do a lot more TV work, I'm more of an all-round entertainer than I was. You have to be, really. It's come full circle in a way, back to how people like Tony

Bennett or Frank Sinatra used to be. Not that I'm comparing myself to Frank Sinatra.

But these days I'm on daytime TV all the time, on shows like *Loose Women*. Kids might laugh at me and Bez on *Gogglebox* and think 'Who are these old blokes?' But they google us and think 'I'll have a listen on Spotify and see what Happy Mondays sound like,' and next thing they're like, 'You know what, these lot are great.'

I'm not the type to use my platform to push my views. I'm happy to help with any charitable causes, like Stand Up to Cancer – and I do a lot of that stuff – but I'm an entertainer not a politician. I prefer not to get into the politics. Unlike Bez, who actually stood in the elections in Salford back in 2015. I wouldn't vote for Bez. He's too much of a loose cannon, he'd change his mind depending on how he felt when he got up each morning. We don't need loose cannons in politics – look at what happened with Trump, the lunatic. These people shouldn't be in power.

When you're in the public eye, the public's first impressions tend to stick, you know what I mean? Me and Bez became famous as the rock'n'roll hell-raisers of the acid house scene, and that's how people still badge us now, over thirty years later. We're known as the ultimate party heads, and that badge sticks, even if our heavy partying days are behind us. Well, my partying days are behind me. I can't speak for Bez. He still gives it a good go, now and then.

In the sixties, *Melody Maker* said 'Would you let your daughter date a Rolling Stone?' and in the nineties the *NME* called us 'the nation's favourite outlaws'. Andrew Loog Oldham, the Stones' manager, knew all that was great for their reputation, and he was proved right. John Lennon was even a bit jealous of the Stones at that stage, because most of the public still saw The Beatles as these clean-cut lovable moptops in suits, even though they were just as badly behaved as the Stones in private. They were shagging left, right and centre, popping pills and LSD and everything. If you read about what they got up to in their Hamburg days, they were nearly as bad as the Mondays, and they were still only teenagers then. But the public perception was that the Stones were the bad boys, and The Beatles were the boys next door.

I can't really complain about having the reputation I have, as we fuelled the fire for a long time, but I do find it a bit boring sometimes if that's all people want to talk about. During the second lockdown in 2020, when we'd all been stuck in the house for ages and everyone was chomping at the bit to get out, there were rumours that they'd invented a vaccine that worked, so obviously everyone was excited, and Nihal Arthanayake on Radio 5 Live told his listeners, 'If this is true, after being locked down for eight months, the whole country is going to want to go out and party like Shaun Ryder and Bez!' That's the first thing people think of when they think of me and Bez. Which is fine. You'd have thought some young kid would have come through and taken the 'Biggest Caner' title from me and Bez over the past few years, but it hasn't happened. We're touching sixty now and somehow we're still seen as the poster boys for caning it. Mind you, Keith Richards is nearly eighty and people still think of him as a caner, even though he's been off the hard stuff for decades now. He was asked about his drug use in the nineties, and he said, 'Even though that was nearly twenty years ago, you cannot convince some people that I'm not a mad drug addict.'

I know exactly how you feel, Keith mate.

When he fell out of that coconut tree, everyone's reaction was 'typical Keith, off his head' and I'm sure there would be a similar reaction if me or Bez fell out of a coconut tree, even though we were stone-cold sober. But the one thing about having a reputation is it makes you stick in people's memory. Would Elton John still be such a huge star if it wasn't for all his ridiculous costumes and the stories about his drug use and tantrums? No way. He had the tunes – don't get me wrong, old Elton can bang a great tune out – but it was all those stories about him that built the Elton John myth. That's one of the main reasons he's bigger than someone like Billy Joel, because there's all these stories to write about that people are fascinated with, and he knows that, and he plays up to it, and I bet he doesn't regret a thing.

Thankfully, these days the Mondays and Black Grape and me are remembered for both things. For the music and the hell-raising. The music has stood the test of time. People still love those Mondays and Black Grape records. Or most of them. To be fair, there's the odd one that I'm not keen on. I'm glad we're not just remembered for caning it. A band like Mötley Crüe are only remembered for the carnage, not for the music. We're now remembered for both, I suppose a bit like the Sex Pistols, or the Stones, although I'm not comparing the Mondays to either of them.

I do Q&As and speaking tours now and I'm like, 'Ask me anything.' I didn't realize, when I first started doing it, that most of these live Q&As are all rehearsed, the same questions every night with rehearsed anecdotes. A bit like the old after-dinner speeches circuit. Whoever was doing the questioning would sometimes ask me to send my questions to them beforehand, but I was like, 'What? Nah... just ask me anything,' because it makes it more interesting for me and the audience. I don't want to go on stage every night telling the same old story about taking drugs, or the pigeon story or something, so just ask me anything and if I can remember I'll tell you – and even if I can't it will probably trigger some tale in there that is hopefully half-relevant to what you're asking, and probably funnier. That's how we did the autobiography a decade ago. At that stage I couldn't remember much from the nineties or the noughties (still a stupid name for a decade, that, you'd have thought they could have come up with something better), but Luke Bainbridge, who I work with on my books, has a better memory than me and does all his research, so when we went over stuff it triggered all sorts of memories, stuff that was hidden down there that I'd completely forgotten about or buried.

Nowadays when I do interviews, or Q&As where fans get to ask questions at the end, there's kind of two different camps. You've got your tabloids, who mostly just want stories about sex, drugs and rock'n'roll. Then you get the *Guardian* or *Times* sort of dude who wants to ask serious questions about songwriting and cultural influences. If I'm doing a live 'audience with Shaun Ryder' I can kind of predict now the sort of questions I'm going to be asked depending on what the venue is. In Manchester, if I'm doing the Bridgewater

Hall, which is the home of the Hallé Orchestra, then there will be more highbrow questions about songwriting and what did I think about being compared to Yeats and stuff like that, but if I'm doing a more rock'n'roll venue like the Academy, then it will be, 'I want to know how much crack you smoked in that wardrobe in LA in 1991!'

People can get a bit over-protective of their favourite bands. It means so much to them. Too much sometimes. They had to set up a telephone helpline for all the fans when Take That split up, for fuck's sake. They didn't have to do that with the Mondays!

It's funny, people feel more strongly about what happens to you when you're in a band than in normal life. You might get married or have a kid or fall out with your family or whatever, but no one's bothered about that as long as the band doesn't change and stays true. Keep it real. Whatever that means. It's weird, sometimes our original fans are the most conservative. They don't want us to change at all. They originally got into us because we were different and challenging the norm, but now they're not happy unless we conform to their idea of what we were thirty years ago. Doesn't make sense. They don't want to drive a car that's the same as the car they had thirty years ago. They don't want to be eating the same food they were eating thirty years ago. Or wearing the same clothes they had thirty years ago. The world's changed in thirty years, but they still want me and Bez to be the same. That's only a few of the hardcore, though. I think most of the fans realize that the Shaun Ryder and Bez characters back then were slightly exaggerated and don't expect us to still be like that all the time now.

I'm not far off sixty now, and I'd never thought I'd get to sixty when I was younger. Mind you, most people back then, if you'd asked them, would have said it would be a miracle if Shaun Ryder made it to forty, let alone sixty. I remember when Bernard Sumner had his thirtieth birthday party at the Haçienda in 1986. I was twenty-three then, and thirty seemed so old. I remember being sat with Bernard going, 'Fucking hell, thirty!… That's *ancient*,' and Bernard turning to me and saying, 'You won't make it to thirty!' I didn't argue with him at the time. But here I am, touching sixty, still in the game.

I still get people coming up to me and saying, 'I can't believe you're still alive!' and I probably always will. To be honest, if I'd carried on partying like I did in my twenties and thirties I'd be dead now. Which is one of the main reasons I stopped. I wanted to hang around, especially for my kids. When I hit forty, I thought, 'Wait a minute, your kids are growing up, you're not young any more, yet you're living the same life you was at eighteen. Get a grip.' Plus, no one wants to be the oldest dude left at the party, that's never a good look. I don't care who you are, if you're a rock star or a bin man, it's pointless for anyone to still be chasing the highs of their youth. Particularly us, who had such highs. What's more, I don't want to any more. I've been straight for years now, and I'm on a different buzz and a different high. I had lots of goes in rehab but it never worked as I wasn't really ready for it. In the end, I did it myself. I did it my way, although I couldn't have done it without my wife, Joanne. She must take a lot of credit for that. When we first got back together I was in the early days of starting to get clean, but not quite there, and she helped me get there and get myself sorted. I remember her telling me, 'You know that feeling you get from drugs that you're always chasing? You know you can get it from real life, if you try?' She was right. It took me a while, but I got there, and I'm happier than ever now.

People ask if I miss the old days. Well, no. Not now, I don't. It *was* brilliant, they were amazing times, incredible times, and we had it right off. We got away with bloody murder sometimes, we really did. I can't believe it myself when I look back. But that was then, and this is now. I like where I am now too. I like having a more chilled life with my family nowadays. I'm also lucky that I came out of it all relatively unscathed. While I definitely partied hard and took lots of drugs, I was never an intravenous user, and I was also lucky to have done a lot of my partying in a rock'n'roll bubble, which is not the real world. A lot of the pals that I grew up with who also partied hard and got into drugs are either doing twenty-one years in prison or they're dead.

I have a healthier life than ever now. It's years since I stopped caning it. I've even stopped smoking, I'm on the vaping. I still have a drink, but mostly when I'm on tour or working. I hardly ever drink at home. When I'm not working and at home, I have a pretty healthy lifestyle. They say you are what you eat. I was a pie for a long time. But now I'm pretty much a pescatarian. Joanne is a great cook, and what she can do with fish and vegetables is amazing.

I'm also more comfortable in my own skin now. More relaxed. When you get to my age you know who you are and what you are and what your disabilities are. My body is a bit fucked because things and old age catch up with you. I used to get out of bed and look from my big toe to my reflection in the mirror and it was hard to tell the difference as my hair had started to fall out due to complications with my thyroid and lack of testosterone! It started to grow back a bit, but it was just like little bits of fluff, so in the end I decided to get a No.1 crop tattooed on. It's called scalp micropigmentation treatment, but they basically tattoo your head so it looks like a skinhead.

Do I have any regrets? Not really. Because I know I behaved like Shaun Ryder and that I reacted in certain situations like Shaun Ryder – and guess what, I am Shaun Ryder. So if I went back and did it all again I'm not sure it would pan out too different. I haven't anything to complain about. We had the time of our lives and I lived to tell the tale, and I'm now happier than I've ever been. Do I wish I remembered more of it? Yes, it would be great to have a picture-perfect memory of what it was like to walk on stage at Glastonbury, or to be headlining the Maracanã stadium in Rio, but I can't remember much about it, and I don't lose any sleep over that. I now know that's linked to my ADHD. I tend to remember snapshots and bits, and when someone reminds me of something sometimes it will come flooding back. But I'm not alone in that, there's loads of rock stars who can't remember a thing. They used to say if you can remember the sixties, you weren't really there, and I'd say that's even more true of the nineties. Ringo has said he can't really remember being in The Beatles half the time. Imagine that. It's one thing me having a sketchy memory of being in the Mondays, but imagine not being able to remember being in The Beatles!

When Oasis played Knebworth it was the biggest gig this country had ever seen, but Noel Gallagher can't really remember it. He says if he closes his eyes now, he genuinely can't remember walking on stage at Knebworth. I know how he feels. I've headlined Glastonbury and I can't remember a thing about it. Weirdly, I remember parts of the weekend quite vividly. I remember the trip down there on the bus, which was eventful. I mean, my memory is not helped by the fact that I spent half the weekend in the baggage hold of the bus, smoking gear. But I do remember doing that. And I remember getting off to our hotel with a girl I'd met on *Top of the Pops*. I just don't remember walking onto the Pyramid Stage for our headline set. I've tried, but there's nothing there. I've got pictures of us doing it. In fact, my mam has got a picture on her kitchen wall of me on stage at Glastonbury, so I know it happened. I just can't remember it. It's not just the drugs for me, or any other rock stars, because it happens to everyone. Maybe it's your senses getting overloaded, that the experience is just too full-on and just too much for your brain to take in at once, so part of it closes down and the adrenaline (and whatever else you've taken) kicks in and you don't remember it properly.

The music industry can be a horrible, dirty business, where it sometimes seems like everyone is out to fuck everyone else over. Hunter S. Thompson famously declared, 'The music business is a cruel and shallow money trench, a long plastic hallway where thieves and pimps run free and good men die like dogs. There's also a negative side.' It's true. It can be a filthy business. I've been fucked over by everyone in my time – by record labels, managers, band mates – but

I've survived. I also half-expected it. I didn't come into the game as some naive kid expecting an easy ride and everyone to have my best interests at heart. Even in *Stardust*, David Essex's character gets fucked over. I knew what I was getting into. I remember when Ian Brown first split up The Stone Roses in 1996, he said, 'Having spent the last ten years in the filthiest business in the universe it's a pleasure to announce the end of The Stone Roses.' He'd had enough and wanted out. Although he soon changed his mind. He said he was going to give it all up and become a gardener and work on the land, but then kids were coming up to him and urging him to go solo and he changed his mind.

I know how Ian felt, there's definitely times when I've had my fill of it. But the good times have more than made up for the bad, for me. I've worked bloody hard, and I'm still working hard, but I've not had a proper job since I was eighteen. I've managed to stay in the game. I think you have to come into this game with your eyes wide open, knowing that at some point people will try and fuck you over, and if you're aware of that there's less chance of it happening.

I never felt any responsibility to be a good role model or anything like that when I was younger, which I'm sure won't surprise anyone. Me, a role model? You must be joking! But I think if you expect *any* rock star to be a role model – now or in the nineties or back in the sixties – you need your head looking at. Same with footballers. Just because someone can write a song or play a guitar or is good at kicking a football, that doesn't mean they have the answers to life, does it? If you stop and think about that for a minute, it's ridiculous. If someone is good at any other job you don't consider them a role model. I'm not a big fan of role models anyway, but I certainly don't buy that rock'n'roll stars or footballers should be role models.

So, no, I didn't feel any responsibility to be a role model. I didn't feel I had to act a certain way because I was the spokesperson of a generation or anything like that. Bollocks. The only responsibility I feel to our fans and audience is to make good records and put on a fucking good show if they come to see us live.

# Myths

People can't get enough of rock'n'roll myths. That's what they want. Outrageous tales of sex and drugs and rock'n'roll. They don't want their rock stars to be clean-living gurus, drinking green tea and doing fucking yoga and Joe Wicks. They want you to be larger than life, doing things they wouldn't dream of doing. They want to live a rock'n'roll lifestyle through you. I was the same before I was in a band, I loved hearing all the classic rock'n'roll stories from the sixties and seventies. That's what made me want to be in a band in the first place. So later on, when the band first started getting attention, and people wanted tales of outrageous debauchery and excess, I was always more than happy to give it to them. When we started the Mondays in the eighties it really felt like we didn't have any true rock'n'roll figures any more. Music, like everything in the eighties, had got all polished and glossy, but it had lost something along the way. It had become *boring*. There was no one causing debauchery and stirring things up like the Sex Pistols, the Stones, the Faces, Led Zeppelin and all those sorts of bands had done. *Top of the Pops* was full of all those Blitz Kids types, like Boy George and Spandau Ballet and Gary Numan, all shiny pop, eyeliner and hairspray. But I knew that there were millions of kids out there like me who wanted some tales of rock'n'roll debauchery, who wanted to see some musicians living the full-on rock'n'roll lifestyle, and if no one else was going to do it I was well up for it. Bring it on.

Half the time it doesn't even matter if the stories are completely true, as long as they *might* be. Did Keith Richards really snort the ashes of his dad after he was cremated? Nobody knows but Keith, but the thing is he *might* have done, and that's enough for most people. That's enough to add fuel to the fire of the legend of Keith Richards. Look at a band like Mötley Crüe and their reputation. Most people have heard of Mötley Crüe because of their rock'n'roll behaviour or because Tommy Lee married Pamela Anderson, but I bet they couldn't name a single record by them. I know I couldn't. I bet even most of the people who bought that Mötley Crüe book *The Dirt* don't own any of their records. They just bought it because it literally dished the dirt on all their rock'n'roll behaviour. Black Sabbath made some great records, but most people only really remember the band because of Ozzy Osborne being off his head all the time, and his wild behaviour, like biting the head off a bat on stage or pissing on that statue. That's what made his legend and helped cement his place in rock history. Even though they made some decent records, Black Sabbath wouldn't have the profile they have now if it wasn't for the myth of Ozzy Osborne.

Tony Wilson, our old boss at Factory Records, used to say, 'When forced to pick between the truth and the legend, print the legend,' and I'm with him on that. When it comes to rock'n'roll, never let the truth get in the way of a fucking good story. People will believe what they want to believe anyway. There would be what used to be called Chinese whispers about what happened around a band, and everyone would tell a slightly different story every time they told someone else, and it just spiralled out of control. There's that old saying that a lie can travel halfway around the world before the truth can get its boots on. That was before social media. It's even worse now. Nowadays a myth can go round the world in a few clicks with people forwarding it on or sharing it or retweeting it or whatever. You can't get too bothered about it.

Some of the biggest rock'n'roll myths are just ridiculous, like the one about Paul McCartney dying in the sixties and being secretly replaced by some other dude. Some people still believe that. They think Macca died in a car crash in 1966 and The Beatles secretly replaced him. These people believe The Beatles left loads of clues, like the photo on the cover of *Abbey Road*, when they're all walking across the zebra crossing and 'Paul' is barefoot, which is a sign of him being dead, and his cigarette is in his wrong hand, and the reg plate of the car on the cover says '28IF' and he would have been twenty-eight if he had lived. Just ridiculous. Even if it was true – if he had died and The Beatles had secretly replaced him – why would they then leave loads of clues about it?! I've met Paul McCartney a couple of times and, trust me, he's still alive. It was me who looked half-dead when we first met at an awards ceremony, not him. This was in the nineties and I wasn't in great shape at the time. It's terrible looking at those pictures of me and him now. He's twenty years older than me, so he must have been in his late fifties then and I was in my late thirties, but he looks much healthier and younger than I do. I look fucked. He must have wondered what I was on. He did once tell a journalist that 'the Mondays remind me of The Beatles in our *Magical Mystery Tour* phase,' which we were all buzzing off. Our drummer, Gaz, even stuck that quote on his wall.

So, yeah, print the myth. Look at Bob Dylan, he was always spreading mistruths and myths about himself. He arrived in New York with a made-up name, and made up his whole back story, saying he'd run away to join the circus and all that. Turned out it was all bollocks, but it's never harmed his career. That all adds to the Dylan myth, trying to separate the truth from the nonsense. It's all smoke and mirrors.

There's so many outrageous stories out there about me and the Mondays and Black Grape, and most of them have an element of truth about them. The 6Music radio presenter Steve Lamacq said, 'There are enough stories about Happy Mondays to keep people talking about them for ever. Bands live on through the myth really, myth and legend.' He's right, and I was always pretty aware of that, even when we were just starting out.

Quite a few of the myths about me and the Mondays and Black Grape didn't happen exactly like people think, but I've long ago given up being bothered about that. Besides, there's even worse stories that people don't know about, trust me. There's also some stories about me that I don't quite understand the fascination with, like the story about me and Bez taking Bernard Sumner's Chinese takeaway out of the bin and eating it, when he was producing one of our early singles. Bernard had only had a few mouthfuls, and we were skint at the time, so me and Bez didn't think twice about fishing it out of the bin and sharing it. I don't see the problem. I'm not sure why people love that story so much. When me and Bez got it out of the bin and started eating it, we certainly weren't thinking, 'Fucking hell, people will still be talking about this in forty years' time!'

Same with the story about me poisoning pigeons so they were all falling out of the sky. That also did happen, but nothing like people think. In the film *24 Hour Party People*, about Factory Records and Manchester, it shows me and our Paul on a rooftop doing it. In reality, it happened when I was a postman, and it was me and another postie. We just got sick of pigeons hassling us when we were eating KFC on our lunch, so we stuck some rat poison in the bread and poisoned the pigeons, who started falling out of the sky. When it happened, I certainly wasn't thinking, 'I tell you what, this will make a great scene in a film one day!' Mind you, anything that happens in *24 Hour Party People* should be taken with a pinch of salt. The character in that film is a caricature of me, it's not the real me. It's a cartoon version of what really happened. I'd obviously never dream of doing anything like that now, but I was a kid at the time. Nowadays, we keep chickens at home, and I enjoy going out and feeding them in the morning and looking after them. I couldn't be further from the kid who poisoned the pigeons. But again, you can't get too worked up about it.

Another of the stories that always gets repeated about me is the one from when we were recording at Eddy Grant's studio in Barbados, and I was supposedly found dragging the sofa out of the studio to sell to a drug dealer for crack cocaine. Yes, it happened, but not quite how it's told. It was a sun lounger, not a sofa. I've even heard one version of the story where Tony Wilson was supposedly on the plane to Barbados and looked out of his plane window as it was coming into land, only to see me and Bez carrying a sofa out of the studio to sell. Do me a favour. For a start, Wilson never even came to visit us in Barbados when we were recording (or supposed to be recording), and as if you can spot someone carrying a sofa, or even a sun lounger, from the window of a fucking plane.

But all these stories have come together to form the Happy Mondays myth, so I really don't let it bother me too much. Even people who were there at the time and witnessed the mad shit that went down have a different version of how it went down. Even me and Bez don't agree on how things happened half the time. You won't be surprised to hear that both me and Bez have slightly hazy memories of what happened back in the days when we were really partying hard. I can remember the sixties and seventies quite well, growing up, before we started the band, but the late eighties and nineties are a bit of a blur, I'm afraid. It's all in there somewhere, my memory just needs to be triggered. Everyone has their own memory of how things happened. Paul McCartney said it used to happen with The Beatles all the time, and he just had to learn to accept that everyone saw and remembered events through their own eyes. 'In an earthquake, you get many different versions of what happened by all the people that saw it,' Macca said, 'and they're all true!'

People love to ask me about the old rock'n'roll clichés. Have you ever thrown a TV out of a window, Shaun? All those old classic rock'n'roll stereotypes. The truth is I've never thrown a TV out of the window. I didn't need to. We never needed to resort to those clichés because there was more than enough chaos and debauchery going on around the Mondays without us having to invent stuff. Stuff just happened to us back then. Chaos seemed to follow us around.

The other main reason we never indulged in stupid pranks like throwing TVs out of windows back in the day is that we never wanted to attract the attention of the police if we could avoid it. We would always be carrying quite a lot of drugs on us – in the early days because we were selling drugs, and later on because I got a habit. If I was carrying heroin, then obviously the last thing I wanted was some arsey hotel manager calling the police because one of the band had launched the contents of his hotel room out of the window and into the swimming pool. So we never threw anything into a hotel pool. In fact, the only time anything did get thrown in a pool at a Mondays event it was by a bloody tabloid journalist. It was at the launch of our third album, *Pills 'n' Thrills and Bellyaches*, at London Zoo. Fucks knows whose idea it was to have the launch party at London Zoo, but it seemed like a good idea at the time. Because the Mondays had become headline news by then, a load of tabloid journalists turned up and they had obviously already decided they wanted a story about outrageous rock'n'roll behaviour. You can read them like a book. They were just hoping for it to turn into a rock'n'roll chimps tea party story so they could use a headline like 'Rock stars behave like animals at the zoo'. One journalist was so desperate to create a scene, to have something to write about, that him and his journalist pal picked up a bench and pushed it over the wall into the penguin enclosure. That then gave the excuse to write the story they had planned all along about the Mondays behaving like animals at the zoo, when it was them who'd done it, the cheeky fuckers. But generally, stuff just happened to us, we didn't need to manufacture it. Especially when we were on tour.

Another of those stories that always crops up is when we first went to New York in 1986 and me and Bez had a gun pulled on us within hours of landing there. That's all true. We'd never been to America before but we'd heard about crack cocaine over there, so the first thing we wanted to do when we landed was try it. We weren't arsed about seeing the Statue of Liberty or Empire State Building or any of the stuff most people want to see when they go to New York for the first time. Looking for crack cocaine was the only sightseeing me and Bez really wanted to do. We were met by a woman who worked for Factory in New York and we asked her to take us to where we could score some crack, but she wouldn't drive all the way there as this was New York in the eighties, when it was still really dangerous. Nothing like it is now. She dropped us a few blocks away and we carried on up, on foot, and met this geezer and got chatting to him and he told us he'd been in Vietnam and he said, 'Come to my crib, man.' He knew we were after scoring. So we went to his crib, in the basement of a nearby building, smoked some crack with him and we were flying. By the time we got back to the hotel, we were still flying and had smoked all the rocks we got off him, so we decided to go back and get some more, but we took a wrong turn and got lost and got surrounded by these street kids. Bez was talking to them, and sometimes when he's off his tits he spits when he's talking. One of these dudes thought I'd spat on him and pulled a gun out and stuck it in my eye. By some miracle, the same Vietnam vet who had sold us the crack earlier that day suddenly appeared out of nowhere and got us out of there.

The next day we had our first ever New York gig at the Limelight, and the manager of the venue – this sexy older woman – took a shine to me and Bez and took us back to her apartment before the gig and gave us this really strong coke. We were absolutely flying again by the time of the gig. Sweating like pigs, eyes on stalks. The rest of the band were wasted as well. Our keyboard player, PD, had to play the gig lying down, he was so fucked. We were that mindless we thought the gig was great, we thought we'd played a blinder, but Tony Wilson was there and he was straight and told us it was the worst gig he'd ever seen us play. So it was our first gig in New York and we blew it a bit, but you get five young lads from Salford and take them to New York for the first time, what do you expect? We were like kids in a sweet shop. Did anyone honestly expect us to get an early night before to make sure we were fresh for the gig?

There was another eventful tour, in France in 1989. The promoter ended up faxing Factory and somehow the fax got reprinted in the press:

I got many problems with the band. First,
they destroyed the hotel in Grenoble.
Second, they didn't want to play the night
of Monday 20th in Paris. I never received
a cancellation for this night. Third, they
got into trouble in a club, Le Palace, in
Paris. Fourth, very big fighting during the
concert of Rennes between the band, the
local promoter and my tour manager Antoine.
Two members of band and crew stayed at the
police station. One of the security went
to hospital (broken shoulder). I saw many
bands (crazy or drug addicts) but never as
dangerous as they were. I can't continue
to promote them in France if they have an
attitude like this.

I do remember that big fight at the Rennes gig. It all kicked off in the middle of our set between our crew and the local crew, so we all just downed instruments, jumped off stage and waded in. I grabbed a big metal pipe from somewhere and was wielding that around my head. Fire extinguishers were going off and all sorts, and everyone got involved. It was a proper Wild West scene, like one of those cartoons where you see a big cloud of dust and arms and legs thrashing out of it. Madness.

We never planned any of that, it just happened, but the press used to lap all that up and it all added to the myth of the Mondays. I'm not saying they followed our example, but Oasis had similar things happen to them when they started.

In their early days, when they'd just been signed, they were on the ferry to Amsterdam to do a gig and ended up in a big fight with a load of football hooligans, got arrested and thrown in the hold of the boat. When they got to Holland, Noel had to phone up Alan McGee to tell him the gig was off as the rest of the band had been deported, and McGee was like, 'Fucking great, man!' because the band were just starting to make a name for themselves and he knew it would add to their myth. Fast-forward thirty years, and McGee now manages me and the Mondays and does a great job. We've both been through similar experiences and really lived the rock'n'roll life, but we're out the other side now and have both given up the hard partying, so he knows where I'm coming from.

A lot of the stories that circulate about the Mondays back in the day were about drugs, that we were selling drugs and were almost like poster boys for this new drug, ecstasy. A lot of those stories were based on some truth, and we didn't exactly avoid the subject. But we weren't any worse than a lot of the kids from Manchester and Salford at that time, it's just that we were the ones who were put in front of middle-class journalists from the *NME* or *Guardian* coming to interview us, and they'd never seen anything like it. There was a time, especially after ecstasy hit, when we were making more money from drugs than the music, not least because we weren't making hardly any money from music at the time and we used to put anything we did make from gigs back into the band. Some nights I would be in the Haçienda and end up with so much cash in my pockets, I had to give handfuls of notes to Leeroy, the manager, and tell him, 'Stick that in the safe, will you, Leeroy? I'll get it off you later.' But that all stopped once the band became successful, even though that reputation followed us around.

Once we got that reputation for being rock'n'roll, it stuck and it was almost like an excuse for anyone who was sucked into our circle to start behaving outrageously. As if being on tour with the Mondays gave you a free pass for behaving badly. It wasn't just naughty lads from back home in Manchester and Salford either, there would be people like Keith Allen, who came along for the ride and the party. Keith was one of the absolute worst of the lot! We met him through Tony Wilson and New Order, as he had just done the England song 'World In Motion' with them for the World Cup in 1990, which was New Order's only No.1. Anyway, after we met Keith, he started coming on tour with us, and he even came on our first big tour of America. He was just into the chaos that surrounded us on the road, but he was much worse than us on that tour, he was completely out of control. We would have been in our late twenties then and Keith was in his late thirties, but he was still hitting it hard, and he'd always be looking to start something. I've been in bars in America with Keith, and he's kicked off for no real reason, just to create a scene, and you'd be lucky to get out alive sometimes. Several times we had to fight our way out of bars or clubs because Keith started something. I've seen him pick up a chair and launch it through a plate-glass window to start a scene. I've never done that. Keith even got it in his head that he was another Bez. He got on stage when we played the Sound Factory in New York and started dancing, but he'd overdone it so much he ended up trying to climb into a flight case by my feet halfway through the gig. Then he woke up by the time of the encore and was up dancing again for 'Wrote For Luck'. He was a lunatic.

We stayed mates with him, and a few years later, when I was living next door to Bez in Glossop, he came up to visit and brought his daughter Lily Allen with him. She obviously went on to be a pop star herself later, but she was still at school then and was only about fourteen. Keith went on a wild night out in Manchester with Bez, and left Lily babysitting Bez's kids. Somehow Keith and Bez ended up in London, still partying – don't ask me how or why – and they didn't get back to Bez's house until three fucking days later. They left poor fourteen-year-old Lily Allen looking after Bez's kids for three days while they were out partying!

There's quite a few legendary tales from our first trip to South America, in 1990, when we headlined the huge Rock in Rio festival in Brazil. We didn't realize quite how big the gig was when we signed up for it. There were nearly 198,000 people, which is a record that still stands in the *Guinness Book of Records*. It was three times the size of Glastonbury at the time and broadcast to 60 million. We'd never been to South America before and took a few journalists with us, including Piers Morgan, who was working at the *Sun* at the time. Other bands wouldn't really talk to the tabloids back then but, the way I saw it, if you're in the tabloids you get an audience of millions, rather than some indie music paper that's read by a few thousand students.

On the plane to Rio, Piers was sat near our keyboard player, Paul Davies, which wasn't a great idea, as PD pulled out a big bag of coke, put a towel over his head and just got stuck in, the daft bastard. On the fucking plane! I did use to wonder if Piers ever had flashbacks to that trip and woke up in a cold sweat, but then when we released the last Black Grape album in 2017, they invited me on to *Good Morning Britain* to talk about the album, and Piers was the one that brought up the Brazil trip and was laughing about it. He said his favourite memory of the trip was when we had a barbecue at Ronnie Biggs' house and Bez gave him a burger: 'I've never found out what he put in those burgers but I had a very, very overexcited eight hours!' I just laughed and said: 'Oh you was *flying*. You was cooking, dude.'

James Brown was the other journalist we took on that trip. James was at the *NME* then and had been an early champion of the Mondays, writing some great reviews of our early London gigs. He's also been clean for years but was still a bit of a caner at the time. I remember on that trip, James kept banging on and on to me about his great idea for a new magazine. To be fair to him, he actually went on and later launched it as *Loaded*, which was a huge success and one of the biggest magazines of the nineties, and he always featured us in there quite a bit. He always knew he could rely on me to give him a great story, and just found us hilarious, particularly Bez. James said recently that one day on that trip to Rio, him and Bez were lying on sun loungers at the hotel, looking up at the sky. Bez squinted and said, 'I want to go up there and do that hang-gliding.' James had to tell him, 'Bez, they're not hang-gliders, they're vultures!'

We never needed to drive a Rolls-Royce into a swimming pool just to create a story, because we wrote a whole fleet of cars off in Barbados. I'm not even joking. The Mondays were sent to Barbados to record our fourth album, *Yes Please!*, and the car-hire firm there had about fifteen cars and we wrote every fucking one of them off in a couple of weeks. Again, we didn't do it on purpose. That sort of stuff just happened to us. I'd jump in one of the hire cars and go out to score and total it on the way back, and then Bez would go out in a different car and total that, and before you knew it, the poor rental-car dude had no fucking cars left. Bez rolled one of the jeeps really badly. It landed on his arm and he ran back to the studio screaming. He ended up having to have an operation where they inserted all these metal bars into his arm to hold it together, but they were all sticking out and his arm looked like the Eiffel Tower or something.

We scared the life out of poor Tina Weymouth and Chris Frantz from Talking Heads, who were producing that album of ours in Barbados. Or trying their best to. They thought they had seen it all, every type of debauchery. Then they met us. Tina later said, 'Coming from the New York scene, we had worked with all kinds of freaks and weirdos, but it was basically a show. They had always turned out to be normal people underneath. I thought that all musicians were the same. When I met the Mondays, I realized that they were different. They were real. They lived that life every day. I never knew such people existed.' She's probably still got post-traumatic stress disorder from it now. Sorry, Tina. Although they did ask me to contribute some vocals for The Heads album a few years later in 1996, which was basically a Talking Heads album without David Byrne, and all different guest vocalists. Funnily enough, they didn't suggest we go back to Barbados to record it!

You can get away with murder as a musician. Rock'n'roll stars are like footballers, you never have to grow up. You have everything done for you, and it encourages you to behave like a kid and to be a bit spoilt. I'm sure I behaved like a bit of a dick at times, but I was never one to throw tantrums like Elton John, ringing up his manager and asking him to do something about the wind outside his hotel. That was when Elton was still doing coke. He'd been up for days and was strung out and, when he finally tried getting his head down, the wind was doing his head in, so he rang up his management and kicked off and told them to do something about it. At least Elton has a laugh at himself. He did a documentary poking fun at himself, called *Tantrums and Tiaras*, and he even talked about that incident recently when he did that *Carpool Karaoke* with James Corden. That's because Elton knows people love stories like that, and it will keep people talking about Elton John, which is what he wants.

Rock'n'roll is built on myths. That's what you buy into when you're a kid. So you just have to go with it. Never start actually believing your own myth, that's when you're in danger of turning into a caricature of yourself and losing touch with reality. You just have to be aware that you're living in a world of smoke and mirrors, and don't get too bothered about it. Stories will get retold and exaggerated and you've just got to learn to fucking roll with it. Chill out. Don't take yourself so seriously.

# Starting a band

The first bit of advice I'd give you about starting a band is: don't talk about starting a band, just do it. Just get on and fucking do it. Loads of people just talk about starting a band but don't do anything about it. It's easy to sit about, talking about starting something with your mates and arguing about what your band name should be and what would you do when you play Glastonbury and blah blah blah. We were the same at first as kids, before we got the Mondays together. It was just me and my cousin Matt at first, and we faffed around a bit with one guitar but never really did anything about it. You just need to go and do it. Anyone can talk a good game. It's like Shane MacGowan wrote in 'Fairytale of New York': 'I could have been someone… well, so could anyone.'

Irvine Welsh said the same thing about authors. He's always getting cornered in pubs and bars by blokes (and it's always blokes) telling him about how they've got the idea for a great book that's going to be ground-breaking, it's going to be the next *Trainspotting* or the next great American novel or whatever. Irvine said that if they were actually a great writer, they'd be at home, writing their great fucking novel instead of propping up the bar and boring everyone stupid about it. The same is true with people who sit around, telling you about the great band they're going to form and how they're going to change the world. There's guys like that in pubs and bars all over the world, boring people stupid. The people who actually start bands aren't in the pub, banging on about it. They're in a rehearsal room or their bedroom with a couple of mates, learning how to play their instruments and bash out a few early tunes.

Back in the day, there was a romantic idea that the best bands are gangs, and they are really. A band should look and act like the last gang in town. A band that has that us-against-the-world mentality that all the best bands have, from The Beatles and the Stones to the Sex Pistols to The Smiths to The Stone Roses to Oasis to Sleaford Mods to some young kids nowadays like Idles. The Mondays were definitely a gang. We were a bunch of outlaws to some people and we were really close-knit, at the start at least. It wasn't just the six of us in the band either – when we moved, we had an entourage. You knew when we turned up somewhere, whether it was a nightclub or a TV station. Then, after the Mondays split and I formed Black Grape, that was another gang, but a looser gang. 'Manchester's Bad Boys Inc', someone called us. Kelly's Heroes. At the time, most of the Britpop bands that were coming through were quite middle-class and shiny and polite, and Black Grape were the hoodlums. We were the naughty kids on the back seat of the bus that everyone was a bit wary of.

A good band should always be more than the sum of their parts. It's what happens when those individual musicians come together that makes them great. That's why when so many great bands split up, the individual members don't really achieve much when they go solo, because it was the chemistry of the group that made them great, not the fact that they were individually good musicians. I don't think some of the Mondays understood that when we originally split up. We'd all fallen out at that stage, but me and Bez still didn't want the band to split. In fact, it was me and Bez that begged them not to give up on it. At that time, I'd have done anything for the band to stay together. But there was a lot of bitterness and they didn't seem to understand that what made the Mondays great was that it needed all of us to make it work. They didn't see that the sum was greater than the parts. I found out later that they were even plotting at one stage to replace me with our bloody roadie, Everton. What a joke.

My dad was in bands a bit when I was younger, and he was always doing something on the circuit, so there was always music around. A bit like Noel and Liam's dad, I suppose, who was a bit of a country-and-western DJ when they were little, before their mam left him. Manchester and Salford was like that in the sixties and the seventies, particularly with the Irish influence, there was always music in the background. I grew up listening to all sorts of music. From rock'n'roll to Irish folk music, country and western to reggae. The Beatles, the Stones, Bowie, Sly and the Family Stone. You name it. I've always had catholic tastes in music. That was one of the things that brought the Mondays together at the start – we all had dead eclectic taste in music. You've got to remember that in the late seventies and early eighties, when we started the band, music was really territorial. You were a mod or a punk or a soul boy or whatever. But we didn't give a shit, we took little bits of all sorts. In the Mondays, we loved Madness and The Specials, sure, but we also loved Dean Martin, The Cult, Frank Sinatra, you name it. There were no boundaries for us.

We got classed as an 'indie band' when we started, and we'd be in the 'indie' section of record shops or in the 'indie' charts in the *NME*, but we never saw ourselves like that. Indie music to us was groups of wet white boys with jingly-jangly guitars and wishy-washy lyrics. Very white, very student. We were never that type of band. We were a rock'n'roll band but with all sorts of influences. We used to listen to a lot of Northern Soul, funk, disco, garage, and then by the early eighties we were already listening to hip-hop and early electro records, which were like acid house before acid house. I thought the best record Factory put out was 'Reach for Love' by Marcel King. That was a huge record to me. We were soaking up all these influences, and they all fed into what we were doing. That's what we would listen to at home, not lots of scratchy indie bands.

Tony Wilson once said Manchester kids have the best record collections, and I'm with him on that. When I was a teenager I used to go round to our cousins', Matt and Pat's, and there would be hundreds of records resting against the wall in the living room, and that's what we vibed off. We'd listen to all those and soak up different influences. Their mum, my aunty Mary, had nine kids and they were all bang into different music and different scenes, and without really realizing it I was taking it all in. It was like a crash course in music and culture. Our Pete was the oldest and had thousands of records, everything from The Flying Burrito Brothers and The Byrds to Captain Beefheart and Link Wray. Our Joe was a skinhead and into soul and ska. Our Mag was into soul and Tamla Motown. Our Gel was into reggae like Bunny Wailer and Gregory Isaacs. Bloody hell, if only our Gel knew back then that years later her little cousin Shaun would get caught smoking crack with Gregory Isaacs backstage at a festival when they were on the same bill! Our Matt and Pat (who later designed the artwork for the Mondays and Black Grape records) were the youngest kids and they were bang into rare soul records, which they used to buy on import. The first albums I got myself were two Bowie albums that I robbed from Scan's superstore in Little Hulton in 1973 when I was eleven – *Pin Ups* and *Hunky Dory*. Then I got Rod Stewart's *Every Picture Tells A Story* with 'Maggie May' and 'Mandolin Wind' on it.

So we were listening to everything from the Sex Pistols to reggae to Northern Soul to Tom fucking Jones, just a big melting pot. Lots of teenagers tend to want to belong to a tribe, to be a mod or a punk or a raver or whatever, but I was never like that. Never just into one type of music. That was one of the things that me and Bez bonded over when we met, that we weren't afraid to say, 'Yeah, we like The Specials but we also dig Showaddywaddy and Tom Jones and Buddy Holly.' That was what bonded us together (well, along with other things), our love of music, and not being frightened to say what you really liked, in case it wasn't 'cool'. Who gives a fuck what is supposed to be cool?

Like I mentioned earlier, seeing *Stardust* was one of the key moments in me deciding I wanted to be in a band. Then seeing Manchester bands like Buzzcocks and Joy Division was really influential. It showed you that lads who had no music background or training could make it in a band. The Mondays just formed naturally. We were all local kids who knew each other or were mates of mates. I was eighteen when we started, and the others were younger. Gaz, our drummer, was only fifteen and still at school. The little sister of my girlfriend at the time was in the same year as him at school, so she introduced us and he seemed all right. I remember thinking, 'OK, he's got a drum kit and he can play the drums and he's got a side parting, Farah trousers and a Pringle jumper... he'll do!' There was none of that putting little notices up in the record shop in town, saying 'Singer wanted' or 'Drummer wanted', with a list of the bands you were into. That's how the rest of Joy Division found Ian Curtis, by sticking up a card in Virgin Records in Manchester. That's how U2 started, by the drummer Larry Mullen Jr putting up a note on his school noticeboard, saying something like 'Drummer seeks musicians to start band' and Bono, the Edge and Adam Clayton all answered.

We started the band in 1981, so we've been together for over forty years now, and obviously I've known our Paul all his life, as he's my little brother, so we've known each other for nearly sixty years. I'm not sure anyone can be mates with someone for forty years and never fall out, and I certainly don't believe anyone who's been in a band for forty years who says they've never fallen out with anyone else in the band. Bollocks. Same as I don't believe those people who say they've been married fifty years and never had an argument. I just find that hard to believe. Everyone falls out now and again.

You get some bands that might as well have a revolving door on the rehearsal room, they change the line-up so often. Mark E. Smith was like that with The Fall, constantly getting rid of people. There can't be many musicians left in Manchester who weren't in The Fall at one stage. But he got away with it because Mark E. Smith *was* The Fall. Most people weren't that arsed who else was in the band that week. Your hardcore fanbase will argue about which line-up of The Fall was the best, but loads of others wouldn't really care who was in the band. Like Mark E. Smith used to say, 'If it's me and your granny on bongos, it's The Fall!'

Joy Division were a huge influence on us when we were starting out. Not necessarily musically, but just to see lads that looked a bit like us up on stage, making records, and on TV. It made it all feel possible. You see David Bowie on *Top of the Pops* as Ziggy Stardust and he looks amazing but he looks like an alien from outer space, he doesn't look like you. But then we saw Joy Division on TV and we were like, 'Hang on, they're just like us.' They made it feel possible. Just having Factory Records in Manchester made things seem possible. You've got to give Tony Wilson and Rob Gretton and Alan Erasmus credit for that. They made a whole generation think things were possible, and think a bit bigger. Johnny Marr says that, by building the Haçienda, Wilson and Factory managed to convince Manchester kids they were living in New York, and I know where he's coming from. I didn't exactly feel like I was growing up in New York, but Factory did make Manchester feel like a place where things could happen, made it feel different from other cities. That's how it happened in Manchester, one band inspired the next. Noel Gallagher said a similar thing about the Mondays to how I felt about Joy Division. He bought one of our first singles, 'Freaky Dancin'', before he even knew what we looked like, probably just because it was on Factory, but when he finally saw a picture of the Mondays he was like 'Wow, they're just like us!' He even said that the first Oasis demo sounds like the Mondays, before they found their own sound and knew where they were going.

When we started it was a case of needs must. The band was decided by what little instruments we had and who could play them. That determined the make-up of the band, really. I never said, 'Right lads, I'm going to be the singer,' but eventually we settled on me singing. All of us had a go, but I was better at it than the others, and when we started trying to write our own songs I was also better at rhyming and coming up with the words. I never demanded to be the singer; we just sort of naturally reached the conclusion in those early rehearsals that I should do it – it just felt right. We played a few cover versions at first, including a couple of Joy Division numbers, as we had to know we could actually play together before we could figure out what we sounded like and try and write our own songs. You have to do some cover versions to know you can all play at the same speed and you're in the right key. So we started doing a couple of Joy

Division tracks, and I'm sure I sounded a bit like Ian Curtis at first, when I was just getting used to singing. I think we might have tried doing an Echo & the Bunnymen track. But no one ever heard that stuff. I didn't want anyone to hear us until we had found our own sound. I think we might have done 'Transmission' at our first ever gig, at the local youth club, but that was only in front of a handful of local kids and I'd be surprised if any of them had heard of Joy Division back then. It wasn't like Joy Division were on the radio, apart from maybe John Peel, and these kids were not the type to stay up listening to John Peel.

Even though in those very early days I probably sounded a little bit like Ian Curtis, especially when we were doing Joy Division covers, I was always looking for my own voice. Like I said before, what's the point of trying to copy someone else? Be yourself, because everyone else is taken. There's no point trying to be Ian Curtis, because Ian Curtis has already been Ian Curtis and he's done a better job of it than me or anyone else could ever do because he *was* Ian Curtis. Look at Bono – he and U2 were huge Joy Division fans, they were in awe of them. Bono said recently that he met Ian Curtis when Joy Division were recording in London with Martin Hannett, and U2 came by to meet Hannett to discuss him working with them. Bono said when he met Ian he nearly freaked out when he was about to shake Ian's hand, and he had this voice in his head saying, 'Oh my god, I'm about to shake Ian Curtis's hand!' That's how much in awe Bono was of Ian Curtis back then. But he didn't copy him and try and be Ian Curtis. He went off and found his own voice and his own way of being a front man, and U2 went on to be massive. They never would have gone on to become the biggest band in the world if Bono was just a second-rate Ian Curtis tribute act.

I knew I wasn't going to be a technically great singer like Sinatra or someone, but I didn't think that mattered when you looked at people like Bob Dylan. People used to say Dylan couldn't sing, but I thought he was a great singer, and it showed me that you didn't have to be technically brilliant, that you could find your own voice and your own way of singing.

Despite being influenced or inspired by bands like Joy Division and Echo & the Bunnymen, we never wanted to ape them, we always wanted to sound like our own thing. Right from the start we wanted to be different. We wanted to be unique. The big mistake a lot of bands make is being inspired by a band that sounds unique, and then trying to sound like them. Bands like The Velvet Underground or Joy Division sound unique, but if you then copy them you're not going to sound unique, are you? You're just going to sound like a Velvets or Joy Division cover band.

We also never tried to be 'hip' or any of that shit. I always thought being 'hip' just meant you were part of a big silly gang of sheep. It's like all these 'hipsters' in Shoreditch or Dalston or Brooklyn now. They're all trying so desperately to look unique, but they all look the same. Thousands of blokes in skinny jeans with sleeve tattoos and beards, thinking they're so unique and have found themselves because they've left Ipswich or Bury St Edmunds and moved to Shoreditch, grown a moustache and started drinking craft beer. Look around you, mate. Everyone in your trendy boozer looks just like you.

I feel the same way about bands who try to jump on any bandwagon, whether it be baggy or acid house, Britpop or whatever. All these bands who try and sound like each other and copy each other's look, they all get lumped in together and then all go out of fashion at once. Some of them could be decent bands as well, but I never felt sorry for them, because at some point they'd decided to take the easy route and jump on the bandwagon. We never tried to do that with the Mondays, or later with Black Grape. In fact, we'd do our best to swerve any music or fashion bandwagon. Like I said, we always had a massive range of musical influences we were drawing from – some that other people considered cool, some that they didn't – but we didn't care what anyone else thought was cool. We honestly didn't give a shit what anyone else thought. If we were into it, we were into it. We were always trying to make something new and original and incorporate all those different styles of music in there. That's why I always found it a bit weird, later, when the Mondays were classed as an indie band. I never saw us like that.

After we got the line-up of the Mondays sorted, we got quite serious about the band quite quickly, in our own way. We were pretty determined. Tony Wilson once said about Joy Division that other bands were on stage because they wanted to be, but Joy Division was on stage because they *had* to be. That's even more true of us. Joy Division all had OK jobs. Ian worked for Macclesfield Council. Bernard worked at Cosgrove Hall, the Manchester animation company that made *Danger Mouse* and *Chorlton and the Wheelies*. (John Squire from The Stone Roses later worked there too.) They might not have liked their jobs that much but at least they had them. The only thing anyone in the Mondays had been was a postman. We were basically unemployable. Who'd employ Bez? Can you imagine his job interview? It would be like when Spud goes for an interview in *Trainspotting*, having a little dab of speed before he goes in, then talking like a washing machine at a million miles an hour. So I was desperate to make it work, and desperate to make it last.

The Mondays were going for a couple of years before Bez joined. He just ended up joining one night at the Haçienda when we were supporting New Order. I'd met Bez through mutual mates. I had a reputation around Salford and so did he. People were always telling me: 'You've got to meet Bez, you and him will get on like a house on fire, he's just like you.' I thought, 'Fuck me, that's the last thing I need in my life... another me,' so I avoided this 'Bez' character for a bit. First time I ever met him he came round my house, but because I was selling gear at the time I didn't want anyone in the house. Before I met him, Bez had been in and out of prison and borstal for robbing a golf club and a house. He then got a magic bus to Greece and spent some time jibbing around Europe, and finally wound up in Morocco, up in the Atlas mountains, where he smoked the strongest weed he'd ever come across, and ended up living in a cave in the mountains with a psychiatrist who'd lost the plot. He was still only twenty-one when I met him, and he'd already done all this mad shit. He was a maniac and a force of nature, and he creates chaos wherever he goes, but he's also infectious – there's a very likeable side to Bez. He can make mates anywhere. Later on, when we were on tour, we'd arrive in some city we'd never been to before and Bez would disappear and by that evening he always had a bunch of new mates he needed to get on the guest list.

Anyway, after we did finally meet properly, we quickly became thick as thieves. He used to come round my house and we'd take acid and watch films. He started hanging around the band a lot, but he didn't end up joining until that night when we were supporting New Order at the Haçienda. Talk about a baptism of fire. New Order were doing two sets and the first one was being filmed for *The Old Grey Whistle Test*. Me and Bez had done some acid before the gig and I was tripping my box off and really didn't want to go on stage on my own, so I just told our manager Phil Saxe and the rest of the band, 'I want Bez on stage with me.' Phil said it would look stupid, but I insisted. That was the first time Bez ever got on stage. He just came up with us and I shoved some maracas in his hand, so it looked a bit better with something in his hand, and that was it. Bez just did his mad dance that he would normally do. He didn't create that dance as part of his stage act, that's actually how he used to dance anyway, when we were out in a club, off our nut. But the thing is, it worked. It gave the audience something different to look at, a focal point, so it worked for them, and it worked for me because it deflected the attention from me. I didn't want people staring at me the whole time. Not just me, though – our Paul used to get stage fright, so having Bez helped him too. It also straight away gave us something that marked us out as different from every other band.

Not everyone got it, though. The funniest thing that happened was the next day some girl came up and said to me, 'Aw, that was nice what you did last night, letting that lad who had special needs on stage with you.' It was just Bez off his nut on acid, and this girl thought he actually had special needs.

Bez was mental back then. He's still on his own trip now, but back then he was off the scale. We played the Haçienda again after he joined, and he fell off the stage in the middle of the set and cut his forehead open. He later wrote about that in his book: 'The doc tells me to take it easy and put my feet up. I thought, "I'm not fucking havin' that." I got some of [lead guitarist] Moose's acid, dripped it in the cut and ran back out with me shakers. Fuckin' raz!'

From day one in the band, like I said, we'd always tried for a unique sound, we didn't want to be pigeonholed. Every album we did we tried to change and do something different. *Bummed* sounds nothing like *Squirrel and G-Man*. *Pills 'n' Thrills* sounds nothing like *Bummed*. The only thing that all the Mondays albums have in common is my voice over the top of it, and weird lyrics.

We did later get associated with the 'Manchester sound', when everything exploded in Manchester, but I always thought that was a bit lazy really. A lazy tag from journalists. All those bands coming out of that Manchester scene then sounded really different. They didn't all sound the same. Yes, there was a Manchester scene, but there wasn't one Manchester sound. The Roses had 'Fools Gold', which had a dance beat, but before that they'd had more of that sixties psychedelia thing going on. The Charlatans came out and maybe had a bit of that baggy Manchester sound, but they had their own groove. No one in their right mind would say that 808 State sound like Inspiral Carpets. They're like chalk and cheese, but they both got lumped under the Manchester banner, when all they had in common really was that they came from Manchester.

If there was a cliché Manchester sound, then that came from the bands who tried to jump on the bandwagon afterwards, people like Candyflip or whoever, who just stuck a dance beat behind the track, or bands like the Soup Dragons, who weren't even from Manchester, they were an indie band from Glasgow, but all of a sudden they're doing dance remixes of their singles. Everyone jumped on it. Like I said before, it's never a good idea to follow fashion or be on any bandwagon, so while everyone was banging on about the 'Manchester sound', we fucked off to Los Angeles to record our next album, *Pills 'n' Thrills and Bellyaches*, and that sounds different again. We were recording in the sunshine and that influenced the sound of the record. You can tell it's been made in the LA sunshine by a group who are kicking back and enjoying themselves, not moping round the rainy streets of Manchester.

When I started Black Grape, it was a different situation. After the Mondays split, I kept it quiet that I wanted a new band. I didn't go round shouting my mouth off about what I was going to do. I kind of knew the sound I was after in my head, and it was just about putting together the people who could make that sound become reality. Everyone had written me off. Everyone. People were looking at what the rest of the Mondays would go and do next, and looking at me as if I was nothing more than just a washed-up junkie. Seriously. But I knew I had the seeds of something special.

I knew I wanted to work with Kermit. That was the starting point. Kermit had been in a rap group called Ruthless Rap

Assassins who were really good, although they hadn't really broken through. We were both using heroin at the time, and the heroin circle in Manchester really wasn't that big, so we met in some dirty back room somewhere. I'd brought him in on the last Mondays album, *Yes Please!*, for someone to bounce ideas off, and that had worked quite well, so I knew I could work with him. Our Paul was involved right at the start, then we fell out and he ended up putting my window through, and that was the end of that. We had Craig Gannon, who had been in The Smiths for a little while, but that didn't work out. We also tried with a couple of the guys from a Manchester band called Intastella, but that never worked out. They couldn't come to rehearsals because they had to go for a meal with their missus or something. I was like, 'Fuck's sake, I'm giving you a real shot here, and you can't be arsed!'

So I decided that Black Grape wasn't going to be a traditional band, as in a fixed group of musicians. It's always been the nucleus of me and Kermit, with a producer – Danny Saber at first, and Youth in recent years – and the rest is loose. Bez was there when he wanted to be, and still is, because that's how it is with Bez, he's got an open invitation. But the rest of the band were all the session lads like Ged Lynch on drums and Wags – that's Paul Wagstaff, who used to be the guitarist in Paris Angels – and they were in place by the time we went in to record our debut album.

I didn't even have a name for the band at first, but what I did have a clear idea of was the vibe I was looking for. In my head, I wanted the new band to be a mix of the more upbeat end of the Mondays, mixed with the party songs of the Rolling Stones, mixed with the stoned hip-hop of

Cypress Hill, who had just come out and were huge at the time. Danny Saber was the perfect producer to help us get that sound, and his input was essential. He'd made his name doing beats for Cypress Hill and he'd been to school with B-Real from the band. They wanted Danny to join Cypress Hill but he wanted to concentrate on production. Gary Kurfirst, who had signed us to his record label, hooked us up and he came to Manchester to see if we could work together. Danny hit it off straight away with me and Kermit. He works really fast, which suits us. He plays bass, so he doesn't wait for anyone to come up with a bass line or beat. He got the beats up and running, so me and Kermit were ready to have at it with the lyrics. The chemistry was really great between all of us in the studio, and you can hear that on the album.

Unfortunately, Kermit later brought in another rapper, Carl, for the second Black Grape album, which changed the chemistry and it didn't work as well, in my opinion. Everything soured a bit, and then people were getting in Kermit and Carl's head, saying, 'You two should go off and do your own thing, fuck the white guy off.' So next thing, Black Grape fell apart because those two went off thinking they were the next Biggie and Tupac. It was history repeating itself for me. Black Grape made the same mistake as the Mondays at the end – certain people getting too big for their boots, not appreciating the huge part the chemistry of the original line-up had played in making the band great, and thinking they could go off and be a bigger star on their own.

So, one of my key bits of advice about starting a band is: once you get going, don't lose sight of what made you a great band in the first place – that's how you start finishing a band.

# Band names

I'd like to give you some really insightful, sage advice on how to choose a brilliant band name, but the truth is that hardly any thought went into either of my band names. I don't think I'm alone in that, though. I think that's probably true of most successful bands. They say the best ideas are simple, and that's true with most of the best band names as well. No need to over-complicate it. Don't choose some obscure reference or some name that's trying too hard to be clever, as right away all you're doing is setting yourself up to only appeal to a niche audience, aren't you? I've never understood bands who set out to be obscure. To me all you're doing is alienating your potential audience before you've started. You might think you're clever being obscure but, trust me, being obscure never sold out the Apollo or got anyone on *Top of the Pops* or paid the rent.

Some of the most successful bands have names that mean nothing, or at least people don't need to get the reference. I'm sure loads of people told The Beatles it was a terrible name when they came up with it. I'm not sure many people got the fact that it was a play on the Beats and beat music. They were called The Quarrymen at first, because they went to Quarry Bank School, then the Silver Beatles, before they settled on The Beatles. But as soon as they made it, you can't imagine them being called anything else, can you? I mean, it's just The Beatles, isn't it? The Rolling Stones is a good name, but they nicked that from the title of a Muddy Waters LP anyway.

Some band names start off jokey but then just take on a life of their own. After Jimmy Page left The Yardbirds he was starting a new band and Keith Moon told Jimmy that his new band was 'gonna go down like a lead balloon', so Jimmy took that and twisted it and ended up calling his new band Led Zeppelin as a play on 'lead balloon'. It didn't do them much harm, did it? They went on to be one of the biggest bands of all time. Pet Shop Boys is a pretty terrible name on paper, so is Arctic Monkeys and Oasis. But now all those bands are successful you can't imagine them being called anything else, can you? That's the thing, once a band becomes successful, the name takes on a life of its own anyway. U2 are named after the form you had to fill out in Ireland to get unemployment benefit, but I bet hardly any of their fans around the world know that. UB40 were the same, that was the old form we had to fill out in the seventies and early eighties. The Smiths came up with their name because it was the most common surname in the country and Morrissey reckoned 'it was time that the ordinary folk of the world showed their faces.' 808 State were named after their drum machine, the Roland TR-808, but if doesn't matter if you don't get that reference, does it? The Stone Roses came up with their name because they wanted something that was hard and beautiful at the same time. Band names that work don't require much thought.

Our Paul says he originally came up with the name Happy Mondays, but I think it was more of a collective effort from us all. In the very, very early days of the band – when we very first started, before we had played any gigs – we called ourselves Avant-Garde at first, then Penguin Dice. I do remember our Paul suggested Happy Loss, after seeing Echo & the Bunnymen on *Top of the Pops*. It came from a lyric in the Bunnymen song 'The Cutter' – 'Am I the happy loss?' – because we were all quite into the Bunnymen when that came out, in 1983. I think Mark Day then came up with the Mondays bit, and we put the two together and it became Happy Mondays. We knew that it was a bit of a cheesy name, a bit childish, but we thought that's the reason it might work, because it was the opposite of what the band were. We didn't want a rough-sounding name that matched the music, we wanted something that jarred with the sound we were making. Apparently, Nirvana later took a similar approach to us. Kurt Cobain didn't want a name that was dirty and grungey like their music, he wanted something that sounded beautiful and magical, like the opposite of the music. Most people don't call us Happy Mondays anyway, they call us the Mondays. 'Are you going to see the Mondays next week?'

Black Grape was an even simpler story. After the Mondays split, I managed to sort a record deal for my new band with Gary Kurfirst in the States. The only problem was I didn't even have a name for my new band. Even by the time we went into Rockfield Studios in Wales to record the debut album we still hadn't come up with a name for the group, and Kurfirst started getting on my case to come up with one. I was like, 'I don't fucking know, mate!' But they needed to announce the record and start thinking about artwork and stuff, so he started pressurizing me for one. 'Shaun, we need a name for the band. You've got to come up with one now!' We were in the studio that day, and I looked up and Kermit had a can of black grape juice in his hand, and I just thought: 'You know what, that's it, we'll call it Black Grape!' and as soon as I said it it just seemed to fit.

I didn't know this at the time, but a pretty similar thing had happened with the Stones. Brian Jones was being hassled on the phone for a name for his new group and was looking down at the floor. He saw the Muddy Waters LP *Rollin' Stone* lying there looking up at him and so he said, 'Er, the Rolling Stones?!'

It's a good idea to make sure someone else hasn't got the same name, which is easier to do now with the internet, otherwise you're just asking for trouble later on. The Charlatans had to change their name to The Charlatans UK when they started going to the States because there had been an American band called The Charlatans in the sixties. The Chemical Brothers were called The Dust Brothers originally, after the sampling production team behind the second Beastie Boys album *Paul's Boutique*, who they were big fans of, but they had to change their name after they started becoming successful. Johnny Marr from The Smiths is actually called John Maher, but he changed the spelling of his surname early on, to avoid confusion with John Maher from Buzzcocks.

# BAND NAMES

If you're signed to a big record label nowadays, there's probably someone in their online team or whatever who would tell you to change your name if it doesn't work very well online or is hard to google. I mean, you're not making life easy for yourself if you call your band The The, are you?

So I'm probably not the best person to come to for advice on band names. But all I'd say is don't go for something too clever and make sure no one else has used the name before. Other than that, if it feels right, just go with it. Doesn't matter if it doesn't make sense on paper, forget about that. Band names take on a life of their own, trust me. Whatever feels right, go with it.

# Rehearsals

When we first started messing around and trying to form a band, it was me, our Paul and our Matt (my cousin who I mentioned earlier), and we would rehearse at our house. Well, I say 'rehearse', but we didn't really do much. Our Paul was figuring out how to play Motown bass lines and our Matt only had three strings on his guitar. I just watched mainly. When Mark Day, who could actually play, joined as guitarist, he said we could rehearse at his mum and dad's house, in the attic. Only problem was it hadn't been converted and you couldn't even stand up properly. Mark's first suggestion for the band name came at those rehearsals. He suggested 'Something In The Attic'. Say what you see, Mark. We used to rehearse once a week, but after a few weeks our Matt left, so it was just me, our Paul and Mark Day, and then Gaz Whelan joined as drummer. Once we had a drummer the noise from rehearsals got a bit much for Mark's mum. I think she thought the ceiling was going to come down, and us with it! Fortunately, Mark's neighbour was the caretaker of the primary school round the corner, All Saints Methodist Church school, which was Gaz's old school, so we started rehearsing there every Thursday. I think they charged us a fiver, and we would use my dad's old PA. It was there that we began to take things a bit more seriously, and rehearsals started to get more frequent. We were still just jamming and feeling our way. The others were trying to work out how to play their instruments (apart from Mark, who was a bit ahead of the rest of us) and I'd be just ad-libbing over the top, talking nonsense half the time, trying to find something that fitted.

None of us could read music apart from Mark when we started. He was the only one who knew about key changes or anything musical. He's still the only one of the Mondays who can read music but, looking back now, I don't think that's massively unusual. When you're starting out, you kind of presume that all professional musicians and any rock star you see on *Top of the Pops* can probably read music and can tell what key anything is in straight away, but a lot of them can't. Even John Lennon and Paul McCartney couldn't read music. When they were recording 'She Loves You', they thought they'd invented a new chord, until George Martin told them, 'Sorry lads, that isn't a new chord!' But that's what makes The Beatles and bands like Joy Division so great, and different – they broke the rules because they didn't really know what the rules were. That's even more true when new technology comes in like samplers or drum machines that allow non-musicians to make music. Like all the young kids in Chicago and Detroit who made the early house music. None of them were trained musicians or knew anything about the traditional rules of making music. They just got their hands on whatever equipment they could – early samplers, drum machines or whatever they could afford – and came at it from a different angle and ended up inventing a new music that changed the world. That's what I always tried to do with the Mondays and then with Black Grape, come up with something different and unique, and why I was really surprised when Britpop came along with loads of bands who just wanted to copy the sound of guitar bands from the sixties. I just thought, 'Really?! Who wants to sound like a sixties tribute band?'

Right from the early days of the Mondays we didn't want loads of people hanging round at rehearsals. We were like, 'Fuck off, everybody else. This is *us*.' We were quite strict about that. People thought we were loonies, locking ourselves away like that, but we were quite determined. We didn't even want my old man there, even though he was really helping us out and setting up the equipment. Once he'd set it up, we'd be like, 'Thanks, but can you fuck off now?' I'm not being awful, but no one wants their dad around while they're trying to become a rock'n'roll band with their mates. I think he was shocked when he came back one week and found us playing our own stuff, rather than cover versions, even though it was really rough and ready.

A little while later, when we met Phil Saxe (who ran the stall we used to buy our jeans off in the underground market) and he started managing us, we got a rehearsal space on Adelphi Street in Salford. It was an old mill, which has been knocked down now. There were loads of disused old mills around Manchester city centre and Salford in the seventies and early eighties, just lying there. It was only about a mile from Manchester city centre, but it was wasteland around there. The whole area has been done up now, but it was still no-man's land in that part of Salford in the late eighties. Now there's artist studios like Islington Mill, Blueprint Studios where Elbow have been based for a long time, loads of new apartments and even the Lowry Hotel, a five-star hotel where Man United and the England team stay, as well as most of the pop stars who play at the Manchester Arena, just round the corner. But back when we were rehearsing round there in the eighties, it really was no-man's land. You wouldn't want to be knocking around there after dark, put it that way. We didn't even realize when we first started rehearsing there, as no one had bothered to mention it to us, but there was a hidden back room where they used to have bare-knuckle fights. One day I had to go and find the geezer who ran the building, to give him his rent, and I went behind the bar and discovered a door in the wall. It was a weird, small door, raised off the ground – you know, like you would get on a ferry or something? I just opened it up and it was like something you see in a film about the Krays or something – a dingy room full of smoke, and two blokes bare-knuckle fighting, really leathering each other, going right at it, and all these geezers stood round betting on it. That's the sort of gaff it was.

Even though it was interesting being neighbours with the bare-knuckle fighters, as soon as we got a chance, we moved to the Boardwalk, a famous live venue in the centre of Manchester that had opened just in the eighties and had a few rehearsal spaces underneath. We took over the room that Simply Red used to have. They'd just had a big hit with 'Money's Too Tight (To Mention)', so had moved on to somewhere a bit bigger and nicer. Funnily enough, Simply Red had got in trouble with the Boardwalk before they moved out because they always used to cover the pockets on the pool table, so the balls wouldn't go down, and they didn't have to keep sticking coins in to play pool. Talk about money's too tight to mention. That's the sort of trick people would normally accuse the Mondays of, not Mick Hucknall and Simply Red!

By the time we moved into the Boardwalk, we had really started taking the band seriously. All the band were on the dole, apart from Mark Day who was still a postman, so we used to rehearse five or six days a week in there, from midday until about 9 p.m. We started at noon as we were never really early risers, and Mark was still a postman so he had to do his bloody round first before he could come to rehearsal. We quickly got much tighter as a band when we moved into the Boardwalk, and that's where we really honed the Mondays sound, I suppose, in those endless days at the Boardwalk. Some people might not have the Mondays down as grafters, but you don't get anywhere unless you put those hours in during the early days. There's actually some early footage of us rehearsing at the Boardwalk on YouTube. Fuck knows where it came from or who put it up there. I know Paul Davis, our original keyboard player, sold a load of demos and stuff to a Mondays fanatic, so it might have come from him. We were probably lucky camera phones didn't exist then, as there would be lots more early footage of us just finding our feet. A couple of years after we moved out of the Boardwalk, Oasis moved in. Noel had joined and they'd changed their name from Rain. They were based there for ages and, like us, that's where they really refined their sound, until they signed their record deal and things took off for them. You can see footage of them playing 'All Around The World' in there on YouTube.

Once your band becomes successful, you get into that cycle of recording and touring, so you're not rehearsing as much as you used to, and eventually we gave up the Boardwalk room. Once you're in that cycle, you only really rehearse before a big tour or a big TV performance or something. You'd never have time otherwise, as you're always on the road or doing the press or doing a TV show or something. Besides, when a band takes off, you spend so much time cooped up with each other you get cabin fever, and the last people you want to see when you come off tour are the rest of the band. You just need a break from each other. It's like that old saying, familiarity breeds contempt. It certainly does when you've been stuck on a tour bus with someone for a couple of weeks.

But in the early days, rehearsing is where you really find your sound and get tight as a band, as a unit. There's no shortcut to getting tight as a band, you have to put the hours in, and the Mondays did. Everyone has to. Oasis did. Joy Division did. U2 did. Even The Beatles had to do it. That's what their Hamburg days were all about, playing in bars for seven or eight hours every night. They were almost endlessly rehearsing, in front of an audience. Then when they came back, they were super tight, a different band to the one that had left Liverpool, ready to take on the world. I don't know any band who's got anywhere without putting those hours in. It's just something you have to do to get tight as a band.

# Clothes and haircuts

Clothes have always been important to me, well before I was in a band. I always wanted to look smart, as far back as I can remember. The first thing I really remember mithering my mam for was a pair of bell-bottom trousers, at the end of the sixties when I was only about seven. Then it wasn't long after that when I saw the Small Faces on *Top of the Pops* and asked her if I could get my hair cut like Steve Marriott, as I mentioned earlier. By the time I reached high school, in the mid-seventies, clothes had become really important to me. In the mid-seventies it was all about Doc Martens, parallel trousers, two-tone trousers, patch pockets, platforms and Royals shoes, which were popular with Northern Soul fans. Looking good and having a good time was what was really important to me, so any money that I managed to get I spent on either some new clobber or on booze. Our Paul would be getting record players or whatever for his birthday or Christmas, but I always wanted clothes. I always had my own look. By the time I was a teenager, I was doing my own thing. I remember getting slagged off for wearing things like a Levi suede jacket with beige Farah kecks but then, a year or two later, everyone else would be getting on that and I'd moved on. By the late seventies, when I was leaving school, I was into what later became known as the Perry Boy look and I started putting my hair in a side parting. That Perry Boy kind of look that we had in the early Mondays years is everywhere now. It's changed a bit over the years, but you can still trace it back to the influence of the Perry Boys.

When we originally started the Mondays we were Perry Boys, and we already looked like a gang really. If you don't know, Perry Boys were the original scally culture and were heavily influenced by football-terrace culture. Hundreds of lads from the North West would go to Europe, supporting Man United or Liverpool, or follow big bands on European tours, selling bootleg T-shirts outside the venues, and all of these lads would bring back continental stuff like Lacoste or Fila. I knew lads who were working all over Europe. Especially Amsterdam. A few of these lads would end up on the Mondays firm later, working for us, or if not working for us then following the band round on tour.

At the end of the seventies and early eighties that was the look... side parting, with a bit of a flick, and a Fred Perry top or, if you were really lucky, a Lacoste top. Mani from The Stone Roses summed it up when he said it made you look like an angel, but an angel with a flick knife. By this stage we were really into clothes and had started shopping at the indoor market in town. There was a shop called Oasis (nothing to do with the high-street chain), which the song on our first album is named after. Noel says Oasis are named after it as well. Liam has said it comes from an Inspiral Carpets tour poster that Noel had on his bedroom wall when he was their roadie and one of the venues was Swindon Oasis, but Noel said, 'In my own head we're the underground market that sells cool trainers, and in his head we're from a leisure centre in Swindon.'

The guy who owned it used to buy clobber off the kids who brought it back from sneak trips abroad. He'd have loads of one-offs in there – trainers that you couldn't get anywhere in this country. Everyone wanted stuff that no one else had, so there were kids who would go abroad specifically on shoplifting trips and then sell the clobber on to places like Oasis. Stuff that was so rare it was like rocking-horse shit. I remember one shop in Manchester having two Fila shirts, which was a massive deal at the time.

That was our look when we started the band, which people didn't really get, but I knew there were thousands of kids like us out there, on the football terraces, out on the town at the weekend, who were on the same vibe and would get it. We didn't need a stylist to get our image, we came fully formed as a band. Our image was our lifestyle. It wasn't manufactured, that was simply how we lived our lives. And we knew there were lads out there like us who had no one to identify with, because we'd had no one to identify with all through the seventies and the glam years. I liked Slade – they had some great tunes – but I certainly didn't want to dress like them, you know what I mean?

The Perry Boys or Pure Boys were the mods of the day

really. International-looking, wearing continental labels, while too many other kids in Manchester were still walking around in raincoats, thinking they were Ian Curtis – you know, that early-eighties Echo & the Bunnymen look, or The Chameleons. That Perry Boy look got adopted by a whole generation really, and it still dominates today. You get shops like Oi Polloi and The End. Their whole look originally comes from that Perry Boy look, and they've done really well out of it. You get lads going in Oi Polloi spending £600 on a jacket just to look like we did when we got all our clobber off the underground market in the eighties.

Phil Saxe later told me he realized there was something going on with our gang of mates. Before he even knew we were in a band, he knew there was a sort of movement from everyone who used to hang around at the underground market and how they were dressed. Then, when he found out we were in a band and starting managing us, he totally got that our look was part of the whole package. He was best mates with Mike Pickering from Factory and the Haçienda and he told Mike, 'I'm going to start a movement with these lads – they look like beatniks, like Shaggy from *Scooby Doo* with little goatees, baggy jumpers and flares.' That was probably the first thing anyone from Factory heard about the Happy Mondays, that we were this bunch of scally beatniks, before they even heard a note of our music.

In 1987, *i-D* magazine tried to get on it and did an article on this new 'scene' in Manchester and called us 'Baldricks'. They actually did two pieces, because they did a follow-up piece in 1988. They called us Baldricks because they reckoned we had haircuts like Baldrick in *Blackadder*. Cheeky bastards.

No one in Manchester called themselves a Baldrick. The lads in Manchester would have called themselves Perry Boys or Pure Boys. In London they would call themselves 'casuals' and Scousers were 'scallies', which ended up being the universal term for boys or casuals. The *i-D* piece talked about the return of flares. We were the first to start wearing flares again, about 1984, but by the time everyone else got on it in 1989 we'd stopped wearing them.

By the time acid house and ecstasy arrived, we'd started growing our hair a bit longer, into a centre parting like curtains, or even a ponytail, and our clothes were also getting a bit looser. If you were dancing all night you wanted looser clothing. I wouldn't dress like that now, but I'm nearly sixty. It's a bit sad if you're nearly sixty and you're still dressing the same as you did when you were twenty.

In the early days we were wearing baggy jeans from the indoor market, but later on when we got a bit of dough we were always quite smart. We never wore Joe Bloggs, for instance. Tony Wilson was friendly with Shami Ahmed, who owned Joe Bloggs, so he got us to do a couple of promo things with them, but I was never into wearing Joe Bloggs. When I see old pics of us in the press, the first thing I look at is what I'm wearing, and most of the time I look all right. I'm wearing stuff that I would wear now. A pair of Armani jeans and a nice top. There's very few pics of us where we're wearing really dated clothes. I was never the type to knock about in a hooded top with a big Aztec design on it. I had quite expensive tastes even back then. I remember we were doing a photoshoot once and our American label gave us 500 dollars each to buy some clothes for it, and I bought an

Armani top that cost almost the whole 500 dollars. The label were expecting me to come back with a whole new outfit but I spent it all on one top.

I've never had a 'stage outfit' as in clothes that I keep especially for performing on stage. I never got changed to go on stage either. If we were on tour and in New York or somewhere and I'd just bought a new top that I really liked, I might stick that on, but usually we just went on stage in what we'd been wearing all day. Bez would sometimes wear shorts because he was dancing non-stop and would get really sweaty, but that was as close to a stage outfit as the Mondays got.

Me and Bez recently did a photoshoot for Palace skateboards, who did a whole range of Mondays-inspired clothing. I get asked to do stuff like that all the time, but half the time I look at the clothes they want me to wear and I'm like, 'Really? You want me to wear this? You do realize I'm nearly sixty?!'

When all my hair fell out a couple of years ago and it was clear it wasn't coming back, someone suggested I get my hair tattooed on my head, so that's what I've done. As I mentioned earlier, it's called scalp micropigmentation treatment. I get it done at a clinic called Skalp in Manchester. They basically tattoo your nugget so it looks like you've just been to the barbers and had a No.1 crop.

# Songwriting

Songwriting is a hard thing to define. Certainly for me, it is. But I also think it's one of those things you shouldn't dissect too much. Don't over-analyze it. If you over-analyze anything then you suck all the fucking feeling out of it. That applies to anything – a song, a film, a book, even a relationship. Put anything under the microscope and examine it to see how it works and you take all the joy out of it. That's what some journalists and academics don't get. They pull everything apart until they've sucked all the joy out of it. My instinct was always: if it feels right, fucking go with it. We were never in a position to intellectualize what we were doing anyway, because we were making it up as we went along. We were just trying to create something unique. We weren't deliberately bending the traditional rules of songwriting, because we didn't have a fucking clue what the traditional rules of songwriting were. But we had an innate sense of when something sounded right, when we had hit on something that was worth working on a bit. Even Bez played a part in that in the early days, in rehearsals, even though he couldn't play an instrument or tell you what a middle C was. He was good at spotting a groove. We were all about finding a groove that felt right, that was our vibe.

When the Mondays first started writing our own songs, we would jam in rehearsals and try and get in a groove and I would just rhyme and ad-lib over the top – little bits of rhymes and nonsense until they started to come together. Quite often the band would get into a loop, possibly because they were off their tits, or sometimes because they knew how to start a song and get into a groove but then couldn't finish it, and I would just freestyle over the top, and a song would emerge from the best bits of that process. I could never teach someone to write a song like me because it's all from instinct and feeling, but it's nice if I hear another artist appreciating stuff I've written. I used to feel uncomfortable about compliments like that, but I'm a bit more comfortable in my own skin and confident now. I collaborated with Robbie Williams during lockdown, and after we did the track he was on Adam Buxton's podcast and told him that, 'Quite often I try and channel Shaun Ryder when I'm writing songs,' which was nice of Rob. Sometimes even I have trouble channelling Shaun Ryder when I'm writing songs!

You get a lot of songwriters saying that songs just come to them like they're magic in the air, and you have to grab them while you can. Keith Richards used to say, 'You don't go after the songs, the songs find you.' Maybe it is like that for some singer-songwriters who are sat on their own with their acoustic guitar and their muse, but that's not me. For a start,

I can't play an instrument, so I've never been sat at home strumming a guitar and coming up with something. I've always written to music. I get inspired by what I'm hearing from the band in the rehearsal studio or the producer in the studio, and I vibe off that. That's my starting point.

Noel Gallagher said he doesn't write the words until the end, and then nine out of ten times they don't come. He said he's got about six albums of songs at home that he couldn't find the words for. I'm the opposite. I don't have six albums of lyrics at home waiting for the right song. I don't have any albums of lyrics at home waiting for the right song. I've never been one to sit at home working on words on my own, then taking finished lyrics to the band. That works for some people but not for me. Different musicians have different approaches. I did use to sometimes have scraps of paper with different phrases that I liked, things I'd heard people say or lines from films or something. I was quite magpie-like in that sense. Noel also said he used to take whole finished songs to Oasis rehearsals in the early days. One night he sat down and played the band the whole second album on an acoustic guitar from start to finish, and that was the first any of them had heard it. That's never happened with the Mondays or Black Grape, the songs always came together in the rehearsals or recording studios.

Ray Davies from The Kinks says that whenever he meets someone new and interesting, he starts writing a song about them in his head, which is quite nice. I don't do that but, if you look back over my songs, I do use certain characters that I've met in my life. I wouldn't write a whole song about someone, but maybe they'll just make a fleeting appearance somewhere.

With Elton John and Bernie Taupin, the lyrics always came before the music. I don't think I've ever written a song that way. Bernie Taupin would write the whole lyrics and then give them to Elton John written down, and Elton would go off and write the music. The Smiths were the opposite. Johnny Marr used to write the music and then give Morrissey a tape with the rough song on, and Morrissey would go home and work on the lyrics that night and come in the next morning with the finished song. Joy Division used to just jam in the studio until one of them, usually Ian Curtis, spotted a bit that he liked and then they'd work on that until they had a song. That's probably closer to the way the Mondays worked than any other approaches.

I do think as a general rule, that the quicker the song comes together, the better it is. It's the same as anything, isn't it? If you have to spend ages labouring over it then you can probably tell with the end result. If it comes out quite naturally it's more likely to sound natural and right to the listener. Some days you might be in the studio and nothing comes, and you have to accept that and just sack it off and go to the pub.

When we started writing our very first songs, they were just full of in-jokes, as we didn't really expect anyone outside of our circle to hear them. There were lots of catchphrases and observations that would have only really made sense to our little gang, plus references to films we were obsessed by. The full title of our first album is *Squirrel and G-Man Twenty Four Hour Party People Plastic Face Carnt Smile (White Out)* and that's all references that only the band knew. People used to call me, Bez and our Paul '24-hour party people' because we were always on it. We'd walk in some place and they'd go, 'Here they are, the 24-hour party people!' Every day was a 24-hour party to us in those days. We used to have a mate called Minny and he popped round to the gaff I used to share with our Paul and Bez one day and we were all a bit munted from too much whizz or coke, and he just laughed at us, 'Fuck me, what's wrong with you lot? Plastic face, can't smile, white out!' Squirrel and G-Man was our keyboard player PD's parents. I had nicknames for everyone back in the day. She was 'Squirrel' because she looked like one, and chewed like one when she ate, and he was 'G-Man' because he was in the police.

Our second album, *Bummed*, is littered with references to the film *Performance* because we had a copy of it on VHS and we were obsessed with it at the time. We only had a handful of films on tape, so you ended up watching the same films over and over when you were stoned, and we got obsessed with *Performance* and adopted bits of the dialogue as our own catchphrases like, 'I like that, turn it up!' One track is even called 'Performance', and another track 'Mad Cyril' is named after a character from *Performance*. *Stardust* was another film that stuck with me, as I mentioned at the start of the book. The line 'You were wet, but you're getting drier' in 'Wrote For Luck' is a nod to the film *Stardust*. Adam Faith visits David Essex when he's made it and he's living in a castle and says to him, 'You're wet!' and Essex goes, 'Yeah, but I'm getting drier.'

Looking back, that all helped create this whole little world around the Mondays that people kind of bought in to. It was like we were painting a picture of our own little world, that people could immerse themselves in.

The song titles often wouldn't come from lyrics. They would also be in-jokes or references to people we knew. 'Olive Oil', 'Tart Tart', 'Cowboy Dave', 'Squirrel', 'G-Man' and 'Fat Neck' were all nicknames for people we knew in real life, although the songs weren't necessarily about them. Fat Neck's real name is Karl Power and he had his own fifteen minutes of fame a few years later when he started doing pranks at sporting events. He wore a United kit and sneaked on the pitch and lined up with the rest of the team before a game. He also jumped onto Centre Court at Wimbledon with his mate's son and had a little rally with him, and the crowd loved it.

Someone like Morrissey or Pet Shop Boys obviously spend a lot of time thinking about clever song titles with double meanings. Ian Curtis probably put a lot of thought into Joy Division song titles, but New Order often didn't seem too. Their songs were usually called something like 'Fast One' or 'New Fast One' until they had to come up with something quick when the record was finished. Stephen Morris said that when they were recording *Technique* he got a parking ticket, and to remind him he had to pay it he stuck a note on the wall in the studio saying 'Fine Time', and then when they were stuck for a name for the opening track, they just ended up calling it 'Fine Time'. It's like 'Yellow' by Coldplay. People think it's this really deep-meaning love song, but Chris Martin admitted recently it's just called 'Yellow' after the *Yellow Pages*. I'm not joking, people think 'Yellow' must mean something heartfelt, but the truth is he was just sat in the studio writing the song, trying to come up with a line at the end of the verse, and he was a bit stuck, then saw the *Yellow Pages* in front of him and went, 'Yellow', and it fitted so he just went with it, and it was the song that really launched their career.

It doesn't really matter where the inspiration comes from. Like I said earlier, if it feels right, just go with it.

# Lyrics

I've never put myself forward as an anguished wordsmith. Where I come from, you don't walk around telling everyone you're a poet when you're growing up. I never even set out to be a lyricist originally. We just wanted to start a band, and I had to start writing lyrics by default because I became the front man of Happy Mondays, and none of the others showed any real interest in the words.

I never placed huge emphasis on the lyrics when we first started the Mondays. I was more concerned about getting the feel and the vibe right for the song. I would have been fine singing lyrics by one of the others, but none of them were ever arsed. If you'd told me back then that one day one of the most famous and respected publishers in the world would ask me if they could print a book of my collected lyrics, I'd have thought you were off your head.

Once the Mondays made it, people talked a lot about my lyrics and I used to get asked a lot about them, which made me a bit uncomfortable at the time. People might find it surprising, but any praise like that made me a bit uneasy. Looking back, I can see now that it's because I wasn't totally confident in myself, like the rest of the band. When you come from a totally untrained background, and you're making it up as you go along at first, you can get a bit of what they call imposter syndrome. But as you get older you can appreciate that being untrained and not knowing what the rules are helps you create something original.

So I would never have put myself up there as a brilliant wordsmith back then. I'm not saying I didn't put any effort into them or think they were important. I did. I just wasn't the type to start shouting from the rooftops about how great my lyrics were. I suppose part of that is down to the fact that I never even knew my alphabet when the band first started, so maybe I was a bit self-conscious. When other people started talking about them, and Tony Wilson started banging on to the press about how I was the greatest poet since Yeats or whatever, I just took it all with a pinch of salt. What else was I supposed to do? Agree with him? I didn't even really know who Yeats was back then. It wasn't the sort of thing they taught at schools in Salford in the sixties and seventies.

Thirty years later, in 2019, Faber approached me and said they wanted to publish a book of my collected lyrics, which I was a bit unsure of at first. But I agreed, and they did a great job with it. Faber is home to loads of famous poets and Nobel laureates – T. S. Eliot, Ted Hughes, Harold Pinter, Sylvia Plath, Samuel Beckett, Seamus Heaney… and now Shaun William Ryder. No doubt that will have tickled Tony Wilson. He was probably up there having a right laugh about that, taking the piss out of Yeats, saying, 'See? I told 'em!' But even after the book, *Wrote For Luck*, was published by that legendary publishing house and got great reviews, I still don't see myself as an anguished wordsmith. I never felt the need to wear my heart on my sleeve like Morrissey. That worked brilliantly for Morrissey, and good on him, but I'm not Morrissey and never will be, and never wanted to be. I always wanted to find my own voice as Shaun William Ryder.

I had always messed around with words and rhymes from a young age. I had a little gang when I was at school, and we would knock about together and set fire to stuff and rob stuff, but we would also make little rhymes up while we were hanging out. Just silly little riddles and poems about 'Miss Annie had a smelly fanny' and stuff like that. Really childish nonsense, just to amuse ourselves. I did write a few rhymes and poems at school but, because I was dyslexic and didn't really know my grammar, I misspelled things and didn't have all the right full stops and commas in the right place. So even though my stories were more creative and original than other kids', they'd get better marks because of their grammar. Or the teachers wouldn't believe I'd written it and accuse me of copying it from other people. I really struggled when I was at school, and when I found out as an adult that I was dyslexic and had ADHD, it made sense and I realized why I had struggled, but back when I was at school there was no real support for kids like me. They didn't even try and diagnose what was wrong, they just dismissed me. It's sad to think how many kids like me were just written off back then. One of my young daughters also suffers from ADHD and it's heartbreaking to watch her go through what

I had to go through, although thankfully there's much more understanding and support nowadays. Who knows how different my life would have been if I'd had teachers who believed in me back then and could recognize that I had some talent, even if it was a bit leftfield. But I didn't. This was the sixties and seventies in Northern comprehensives, and teachers didn't really encourage you. No one at our school was given that belief. This was when they called Reading, Writing and Arithmetic 'the three Rs', which is a bit of a stupid thing to teach kids as only one of those three actually begins with R anyway! That's just taking the piss out of people who are a bit dyslexic like me.

When I realized that I was going to be punished at school for not conforming to their idea of what good writing was, I just stopped writing my little stories and thought 'Fuck it' and became a bit of a joker and a tearaway. It's really sad, when you think how many kids of my generation that happened to. Most of them never found a creative outlet later, and just ended up doing dead-end jobs through no fault of their own, when they were capable of so much more.

So I'm self-educated really. Everything I know is self-learned. 'Autodidact' they call it apparently – that means someone who is self-taught. I wasn't a big reader when I was a kid. The only books I read were the *Skinhead* and *Suedehead* books by Richard Allen, which were like little skinhead pulp fiction novels that were really popular in the seventies, but even then I would look at the covers, then just skip to the bits where there was swearing and shagging. I'm still not a huge reader, I'm more self-taught from films and documentaries, and also from endless late-night conversations after a night out, at some after-hours club or back at someone's house, staying up all night into the next day. I'll soak all that in. It wasn't all just about getting mindless back in the day – I'd get into conversations and debates with certain people that turned you on to different things or made you think about things in a different way. Even someone like Tony Wilson, who went to Cambridge, I could hold my own with and have a fascinating conversation with and we'd vibe off each other. I might not have read all the classics, but I always had an open, inquisitive mind. I used to like watching *The Learning Zone* on BBC2 when it was on late at night, and then later on a lot of Sky News. Now I watch a lot of the History channel and Discovery Channel, things like that.

One of the first songs I wrote was called 'Saigon', about the Vietnam war. I didn't really know anything about the Vietnam war, but we watched a lot of Vietnam films like *The Deer Hunter* and *Apocalypse Now*. The lyrics were something like 'From the size of a needle locked in your arm to the Russian roulette and the funny farm in the back streets of old Saigon'. Gaz and the rest of the band thought it was great, but I hated it. I used to cringe at the lyrics.

Quite a few of those early songs I still cringe at. For me, it just sounds like us finding our feet in public. I don't think those very early songs should really have been recorded and put out because we weren't ready. I was still finding my voice. I'm not sure any of the early stuff should have seen the light of day until 'Tart Tart', really. But some other people disagree, and a couple of years ago London Records rereleased a luxury edition of our early EPs thirty-five years after they were recorded. They even got Pete Fowler, who does all the

Super Furry Animals artwork, to do a great animated video for 'The Egg', so obviously not everyone agrees with me. 'The Egg' was a bright-yellow car our Paul had back then. It was the same colour as an egg yolk, so we just nicknamed it 'The Egg'. People would see me and our Paul coming and go, 'Here's the 24-Hour Party People, in The Egg.'

Lyrics are not really designed to be dissected on the page like poetry, as sometimes they don't make much sense when you take them away from the music. I think a lot of it is about what feels right for the song, for the vibe. When I'm writing lyrics in the studio I would ad-lib and talk nonsense at first until I got the vibe and melody that suited the song, and then would often keep changing the lyrics around a bit each time we played it, so often there wasn't even a finalized version of lyrics, really.

Some academics and journalists really do go a bit overboard on analyzing lyrics. Some professor wrote a whole book analyzing the lyrics of 'Eleanor Rigby', for fucks sake! Does anyone want a whole book on the lyrics of 'Eleanor Rigby'? Talk about writing the words of a sermon that no one will hear.

I've never really read anyone else's lyrics for inspiration. I would listen out for lyrics in songs but, you know how it is, no matter how much you think you've heard the words correctly, when you see them written down you realize you've been singing the wrong words all your life. I do have ADHD as well, so I have to try really hard to concentrate and focus if I'm listening to lyrics. Otherwise I'll find myself drifting off and following the bass line instead. I always misheard lyrics anyway, but I'm not the only one. Apparently when the songwriter Bobby Hart first heard 'Paperback Writer' by The Beatles on the radio he thought they were singing 'Take the last train' in the chorus. By the time someone told him they were singing 'paperback writer', that was already stuck in his head. Then he was asked to write a song for The Monkees, so he took that misheard lyric and turned it into a song, and the first line of the song was 'Take the last train... to Clarksville'. It ended up going to No.1 on the US charts for The Monkees, all from a misheard lyric. Peter Kay does a whole routine about people singing the wrong lyrics, dancing to Abba at weddings, singing: 'Dancing Queen, feel the meat, of the tangerine...'

I've had people coming up to me, misquoting my lyrics to me. One guy almost got a bit aggro with me, this big Serbian dude. He came right up to me and was like, 'What have you got against Serbs?' I said, 'What you on about, mate? I haven't got anything against Serbs. I don't think I've even met a Serb before!' He said, 'Why do Black Grape sing, "Most of these men sink like Serbs"?' I was like, 'It's "subs", mate! "Most of these men sink like subs!" It's short for submarines – you know, *glug, glug, glug*!'

Very few of my songs are about one single thing. Most of them are a collection of different incidents or scenes. I write in pictures, so I'm just describing what I see in my mind really. I'll get a mad scene in my head and I'm just painting a picture of that story. It's almost like there's a mad oddball cartoon running through my head and I'm like a commentator on that scene, describing it as it plays out. I also used a lot of our own language and slang and in-jokes as well. Salford has its own language and catchphrases and odd ways with words. We'd talk about 'doing one' or 'things coming on top', which means when things are getting a bit moody or getting out of hand. Anthony Burgess, who wrote *A Clockwork Orange*, was a Salford kid, and some of that Salford way with language is definitely there in *A Clockwork Orange* in the way Alex and his gang talk, with their own slang and little catchphrases.

Some people used to assume that the way I wrote was partly down to drug use, and maybe even I thought that a little at the time. That I needed drugs to help unlock those stories and write. But now I'm older I can see that wasn't really the case. That's just how my mind naturally works and sees things. That's how the world looks to me. Partly my ADHD, partly because I'm self-taught and mainly because that's how I'm wired inside. That's how I put those first stories and rhymes together when I was a kid, long before I'd touched any drugs, and I write in a similar way now, long after I became clean.

A lot of lyrics are open to interpretation. I'm not one of those lyricists who are adamant about what songs are about, and 'it doesn't mean this, it means that'. Let people have their own interpretations of it. If I'm playing a gig to 10,000 people, they might have 10,000 different interpretations of the song I'm singing, which could depend on when and where they first heard it. One of them might take one lyric and go down a rabbit hole about what that means, and some other dude has focused on another lyric and the song means something totally different, and maybe a song doesn't mean anything to most of them. There's plenty of songs by other bands that I'm into that I'm pretty sure I know what they're about, and others I've not really thought what they're about.

If I was interviewed back in the day, depending on what mood I was in, I might say a song was about something more specific, about this or that, when it wasn't really. Sometimes the songs were a little more abstract or surreal, just words that sounded good and created an image in my brain when I was stringing them together. Half the time I was more concerned with how the words sounded than with what they actually meant. I would sing slightly different lyrics each night, and what ended up on record was only the version that I sang that day. I still tweak them and ad-lib them a bit now. That's one of the weirdest things about doing the lyric book: most of my lyrics were never set in stone.

I would sometimes incorporate little nursery rhymes or phrases into my lyrics, like 'Henny Penny, Cocky Locky, Juicy Lucy, Turkey Lurkey, Chicken Licken' or things like that. I didn't know this at the time, but John Lennon sometimes used to do that as well. Half of 'I Am The Walrus' is taken from a children's rhyme from the 1950s called 'Dead Dog's Eye' that Lennon remembered singing as a kid in the school playground with his mates.

Yellow matter custard, green slop pie
All mixed together with a dead dog's eye
Slap it on a butty, ten foot thick
Then wash it all down with a cup of cold sick.

He also nicked the Walrus in 'I Am The Walrus' from *Alice in Wonderland*, apparently. Come to think of it, 'I Am The Walrus' was on The Beatles' *Magical Mystery Tour* album, so maybe that explains where Paul McCartney was coming from later, when he said that the Mondays reminded him of The Beatles in their *Magical Mystery Tour* phase.

One of my most famous lyrics that people pick up on is 'Son, I'm thirty/I only went with your mother's cos she's dirty', which is the opening line from 'Kinky Afro', but that was just a bit of a throwaway line that stuck. Just the sort of thing I'd come up with when I was ad-libbing in the studio, that maybe you don't plan on keeping at first, but then it fits the song so neatly that you end up keeping it. I wasn't even thirty at the time! I was only twenty-eight, but 'Son, I'm twenty-eight/I only went with your mother cos she's a mate' or 'Son, I'm thirty-four/I only went with your mother cos she's a whore' wouldn't have worked nearly as well. I certainly didn't think when I first came up with it in the studio that people would still be quoting the lyric back to me when I was sixty! But you never do think like that. You'd never finish anything if you were always worrying about what it would sound like in thirty years' time. You just go with what feels and sounds right at the time.

I never had any of my lyrics actually banned, although I did annoy a few people, including the Catholic church. There's a line in 'Kuff Dam' from the first Mondays album that I'd never write now: 'You see that Jesus was a cunt/And never helped you with a thing that you do'. I wouldn't dream of writing something like that now, but back then I didn't care. Like I said, I wasn't worrying about how it would sound in thirty years' time – or even thirty days' time – it just felt right at the time. It wasn't exactly radio-friendly, although we weren't getting much radio play anyway at that stage, and it wasn't a single. We did record it for John Peel when he asked us to do a session and I changed the words.

The one time we did have an issue with lyrics with the BBC was when we released 'Loose Fit' as a single from *Pills 'n' Thrills*. The Gulf War was at its height, so there was an issue with the BBC about the lyrics 'Gonna build an air force base/Gonna wipe out your race' and 'Kill who you're killing', although obviously the song wasn't written about the Gulf War. We just had to postpone the single while an edit was done for radio. We weren't the only ones who had issues – Massive Attack had to drop 'Attack' from their name and just become 'Massive' temporarily.

Apparently, the Roman Catholic church weren't too happy with Black Grape's debut single, 'Reverend Black Grape' and the lines 'Old Pope he got the Nazis/To clean up their messes/In exchange for gold and paintings/He gave them new addresses'. They never complained to me or the record label, but some journalist tried to get a response from the Pope about that line, and the spokesperson for the Vatican said, 'Oh dear. Well, I mean, there's nothing I can say about that.'

# Record labels

I 've been on a whole load of different record labels throughout my career, and I had different experiences with each of them. The Mondays will obviously always be closely associated with Factory, which is one of the most famous and influential independent record labels of recent times. But I've also been on MCA, Radioactive, London Records, and most famously – or infamously – had a meeting with EMI where they were offering us a million-pound deal but I walked out to get some KFC or heroin, depending on what version of the story you've been told or want to believe. Not strictly true, but we'll get to that in a bit.

We didn't fully appreciate it at the time – because you don't as a kid, you're too busy trying to get your own band going and make it – but, looking back, Factory was really important. Joy Division, New Order and Factory inspired kids from Manchester and Salford to think that being in a band was possible, and it was possible to make a living doing something creative. As did other independent bands from Manchester like Buzzcocks and The Smiths. Tony Wilson was never shy of bigging up Factory and he said it made kids think differently about where they were from and what was possible. His argument was that if the most important thing to you is rock'n'roll, and when it comes to rock'n'roll your hometown is more important than Tokyo and Paris and up there with New York, then how can you live in a shithole? It made you think you lived somewhere where you could make things happen. If you're knocking about town and running into people who are making records and on *Top of the Pops*, then it suddenly doesn't seem like an alien thing to do. It makes it seem more achievable. Hopefully kids still feel like that today. The Mondays might not always have been the best role models for young kids, but we might have given the younger generation hope, that if we were able to put a band together, get on *Top of the Pops*, play stadiums and tour the world, then they could do it too.

I don't know what would have happened to the Mondays if we hadn't signed to Factory back in the day, as there weren't really any other big independent labels in Manchester at the time, and it's hard to see a major label in London taking a gamble on the early Mondays. I mean, half of Factory couldn't get their heads round the Mondays at first, so it's hard to imagine some bigwig in a suit at EMI or Sony getting it.

We did have one label who came up from London to see us before we signed to Factory. We had sent our demo down and they came up to see us, but they took one look at us and said that we needed an 'image'. They couldn't see us making it as we didn't have an image. This was the mid-eighties, when big acts were bands like Culture Club, Wham! and Eurythmics, and then Frankie Goes to Hollywood and Dead or Alive. It was as if they wanted me or Bez to start dressing like Boy George or Pete Burns. Imagine that. We were like, 'Fuck that, this *is* our image.'

That was our first experience of how A&R – artists and repertoire – at a record label just don't get it half the time. Back in the day, it was A&R men (and it was almost always blokes) and the A&R department who signed bands and would then oversee their 'development' and recording. Basically, they'd convince the label that they should sign you, and then it was their job to make sure you sold records for the record company. When you signed a deal, you'd get an advance, a big lump of cash (well, hopefully a big lump!) and then you had to make that money back for the record company, to 'earn back your advance', before you started making any more money. Loads of other things would be taken off that, like recording costs and touring costs. That's where loads of bands fuck up, they don't see that as their money. They think it's the record company's money. You might be on tour, staying in hotels that are getting paid for, on a tour bus that is getting paid for, getting PDs (*Per Diem* – that's an amount of cash given to each member of the band and crew each day on tour to pay for your expenses – you might get £30 or £50 PDs, depending on how expensive the country you're in is) and having a rider of food and booze, and the tour manager has got petty cash or a record-company credit card to pay for anything else you need, and you're thinking, 'This is all right, someone else is paying for everything.' But what a lot of bands don't realize is that's all *your* money and you're the one who's ultimately paying for it most of the time.

People might think we landed our first record deal really easily, but it certainly didn't feel like that at the time. When we first started the band, we had no idea how to even get a gig in Manchester, let alone get our foot in the door at Factory Records. We had no contacts in the music industry at all, we didn't know anyone. Obviously, when we were growing up, we'd watched how Factory had started with Joy Division, and we were all really into Joy Division. Like I said, some of the first songs we ever tried to play when we were trying to form a band were Joy Division songs. Because me and our Paul were working at the Post Office at the time, he'd managed to get hold of Hooky's home address in Salford, and he'd gone down there and took one of our first demo tapes and stuck it through Hooky's door, but he never got in touch with us and we didn't know if he'd even got it. I've heard Hooky say that was how Factory first got on to us as a band, and Bez reckons Hooky even said that we all turned up at his house, and he just saw a load of ruffians and he panicked and said, 'I haven't got any money, lads. Now do one!' but that definitely isn't true!

In the end, we got introduced to Factory through Phil Saxe, who we got chatting to at his stall on the underground market in Manchester where we used to buy our jeans because they sold the widest flares. We told him we were in a band, and gave him a demo tape. What we didn't know at the time was that Phil was best mates with Tony Wilson, Alan Erasmus and Mike Pickering from Factory. We probably didn't even know who Alan and Mike were at that time, to be honest. Tony Wilson was the public face of Factory Records, and everyone knew him because he was on TV every night, but most people didn't know who the rest of Factory Records were. It was a huge stroke of luck because Phil went and had a word with Factory and said, 'Have a listen to this, help these lads out.' But then it was up to us. It's like anything, isn't it? You can get lucky by meeting someone who knows which door to knock on for you, but once you've got your foot in the door you've got to prove yourself or you're straight back out the door.

Phil was banging on to Mike about us as a band and how we were part of a movement, and Mike's ears pricked up so he came down to see us do a gig at a youth club in Salford. Mike was the booker at the Haçienda and later became the resident DJ who brought in acid house. He thought we were raw and I sounded like Fergal Sharkey (he told us later!) but he was really into the vibe and thought he should sign us to Factory. Mike's version is he then went to Tony and said, 'I've got this band, Happy Mondays,' and Tony just said, 'Darling, you want to sign them, then you sign them.' Rob Gretton – one of the other directors of Factory, and New Order's manager – wanted to see us first, which was why we got the New Order support gigs, but Rob was into us as well.

We were lucky in that, as soon as Tony met us, he loved us. He loved the sort of gang mentality we had, he loved that we were a bit rough. Factory had all been born out of Tony and everyone else seeing the Sex Pistols at the Lesser Free Trade Hall in 1976. Tony saw himself as a bit of a Malcolm McLaren figure, and I think he came to see us as his Sex

Pistols, in a way. Not that we sounded like the Pistols – we never wanted to be a punk band – more that we were his rough outlaws of a band and he could play the Svengali, in his mind. Funnily enough, I remember when I first saw Tony when I was a teenager at a gig at Belle Vue, and my gut reaction was to throw a pint of beer at him. People who live in London or other parts of the country think of Wilson as this record-company dude who signed Joy Division, but to us he was also the guy on the local news each night.

As soon as we were with Factory, we started going to the Haçienda more because we could get in for free. It was still empty but Mike Pickering wanted to get more people like us in there to change the vibe. The Haçienda was launched by New Order and Factory in 1982, inspired by the clubs they'd been to in New York. Tony had found the name from some old French situationist called Ivan Chtcheglov who said, 'We are bored in the city, there is no longer any temple to the sun... you'll never see the Haçienda. It doesn't exist. The Haçienda must be built.'

After it was built, someone said to Tony, 'Who have you built this for?' And he said, 'Well, the kids...' And they said, 'Have you seen the kids? They're walking round in big overcoats and you've built them a New York discotheque.' But Factory were proved right. Wilson called it 'Praxis' later, which is another of his words that no one else used or knew what it meant, but praxis basically means you work out the meaning of what you're doing while you're doing it. Which I suppose you could apply to my whole life.

Factory were an independent record label, but it was the biggest independent of the eighties, thanks to Joy

Division and New Order. A bit like Granada was the greatest independent TV company at the time. People thought it was great that Wilson never went to London, and stayed in Manchester, but they forget that he was working for the best TV channel in the country at the time. Granada, in Manchester. It's not like Granada was holding Wilson back. No other channel would have had the balls to let him create shows like *So It Goes* and put the Sex Pistols, Iggy Pop and new bands like Joy Division on the TV.

There is this myth that still exists that Happy Mondays brought down Factory Records, but that's bollocks. It wasn't us, or New Order. Factory Records brought down Factory Records. The Haçienda was dead until our little gang got on it and brought thousands of people through the door, rammed it to the rafters. Factory owed us money for ages, not the other way round. What brought Factory down was spending a fortune on a stupid new office, and the fact that they didn't own the building the Haçienda was in. Plus they kept spending 100 grand here and 200 grand there on loads of bands who couldn't get arrested. That's what brought Factory down, all that money that was wasted on bands like The Adventure Babies, Cath Carroll and The Wendys. Some of them were OK, but they were never going to make back the money that Factory spent on them. Eric Longley, who was the accountant and then managing director of Factory, reckons they spent over £250,000 just on Cath Carroll, and she sold less than 4000 records. Do you know what I mean? You do the maths.

New Order hadn't released a record for four years, and during that time we'd been the only band on the label who actually made Factory any money. Our manager Nathan McGough said at the time, 'If anything, we've kept Factory going for the past two years.' I remember being in some dive bar in America and I went for a piss and even there someone had scrawled 'Shaun Ryder has ruined Factory' on the wall. I just had to laugh at that. It was nonsense but a typical Factory myth – why let the truth get in the way of a good story?

Don't forget, Factory had also missed out on bands like The Smiths and Oasis. Noel took the first Oasis demo in to Phil Saxe at Factory, our old manager, who was then head of A&R, and he said they would send someone to see their gig the next week, but they never turned up. Apparently they thought Oasis were 'too baggy'. Factory had also pretty much ignored the acid house revolution that was happening under their noses in the Haçienda. In the end, Mike Pickering got so pissed off at Factory not getting dance music that he went off and did Deconstruction Records on the side, and had big hits with bands like K-Klass and the Bassheads, and even signed Kylie Minogue. He put out Black Box's 'Ride on Time' and was having a pint with Alan Erasmus from Factory in Dry Bar when it was at No.1, and Alan said, 'These records that everyone goes mad to at the club, who puts them out?' and Mike was like, 'I put them out, on this other label called Deconstruction.' And Alan was like, 'Why are we not putting them out? You work here. That's a bit silly, isn't it?' It had just passed Factory by. At the time, they were more interested in starting Factory Classical, who sold about twenty records. So it's a total myth that the Mondays brought down Factory Records.

The other issue was they had started handing out cash to all these bands, whereas before no one had got anything.

None of the bands in the eighties had got big advances, not even Joy Division or New Order, and we certainly didn't. You got paid bit by bit, and New Order always had problems getting money out of Factory, as did we once we became successful. It was always Factory that owed us money, not the other way round. But then, after we became successful and they had us and New Order both doing well, and the Haçienda took off, then they got ahead of themselves and started handing out big advances to all these bands that were never going to make that money back. It's crazy, looking back. The Adventure Babies probably got a bigger advance from Factory than Joy Division, New Order and Happy Mondays combined. Mental.

Part of it was because they got ahead of themselves and got a bit giddy, and part of it was the knock-on effect of all the other record companies sniffing around any band from Manchester. When the Manchester thing exploded, there was a little period where every record company wanted a slice of the Manchester vibe, and it felt like every A&R man in London had been stuck on the train to Manchester and told not to come back until they'd signed a Manchester band. So pretty average bands who'd only been going two minutes were getting offered silly advances when they'd only played one gig and not even written five songs yet. I guess Factory thought they had to compete with that and start paying out a bit of cash. But they'd never done that before. A lot of those silly mistakes were bankrolled by *Technique* and *Pills 'n' Thrills*, by us and New Order.

We were on Factory in the UK, but we had a different record label in the States. Over there we were signed to

Elektra, which we thought was cool because it was home of The Doors, Love, The Stooges, MC5 and loads of cool American bands. When we did our first big US tour, Elektra were really excited and spent a load of money on promoting it. The main guy at Elektra then, the president and CEO, was Bob Krasnow, who was in his fifties and was the guy who had originally signed Captain Beefheart. He had worked with everyone, from Ike and Tina Turner, Marc Bolan and T. Rex, Arthur Lee and Love, Kraftwerk to The Cure. He'd also been one of the founders of the Rock & Roll Hall of Fame with Ahmet Ertegun, Seymour Stein and Jann Wenner from *Rolling Stone* magazine. So he was one of the major dudes in the music industry, but I really got on with him, he was sound. Although I was a bit taken aback when me and Bez first went to meet him and he told Nathan, our manager, afterwards: 'They both seem like nice guys, but that guy Shaun – I can't understand a word he's saying, man.'

Nathan was laughing: 'What, but you can understand Bez?!'

'Yes, I can understand Mark, is it? Bez? Yeah, I can understand him, but I can't understand Shaun.'

I thought: 'Fuck me, most of the English can't understand Bez!' He wasn't the only American to feel like that, though. When me and Bez first started doing interviews on American TV they gave us subtitles, the cheeky bastards. We found it funny, watching ourselves on MTV with subtitles.

One of the myths about the collapse of Factory Records and the Mondays imploding was it was all down to me walking out of the meeting with EMI's head of A&R, Clive Black, to get some KFC or to score some heroin, depending on which story you believe. Like that meeting was going to save Factory Records and the Mondays, and I was the one that scuppered it all. That's not the whole story. What usually gets missed out was that all the new music they played Clive Black was instrumentals, which he was less than impressed with, because our sound man had conveniently lost my vocal tracks. But also the fact that Clive had realized Factory didn't actually own all the back catalogue, which is what he was really interested in. When they started Factory, Wilson wanted the label geared towards supporting the artists, so they pioneered the 50/50 profits split between label and artists and had a 'non-contract', which meant the artists owned their own recordings, which no other label would do. After Factory went down, Wilson later said, 'That document that states "We own nothing. The musicians own everything" in the end made Factory bankrupt, and resulted in my entire catalogue being owned by somebody else. But I can't regret it, because the idea was not to own the past but to present the future.'

'Sunshine and Love' was then scheduled to come out as the second single from the album, but then that got delayed for a few weeks because Factory didn't have the cash to pay for the actual record to be pressed and couldn't find a record-pressing plant that would give them credit any more. That's how dire the situation had got for Factory in 1992. They didn't have a pot to piss in, and everyone knew it so wanted paying up front. Factory were so broke at this stage that Tony was scrabbling around, trying to borrow money to make a video for the single. I remember Tony getting pissed off at me because I didn't really put any effort into promoting the single, but I just didn't believe in the record so I couldn't bring myself to do it. The whole situation was getting toxic by that stage.

When Factory finally went under, a couple of weeks later, it was obviously really sad but it had become inevitable. It didn't just happen one day; it was dragged out for a few weeks, probably months, and the writing had been on the wall for at least a year.

When the Mondays split, everyone wrote me off. Even Wilson, who had been my biggest champion. But, unbeknown to everyone, I was soon on a flight to the States to sort a new record deal with Gary Kurfirst (who had signed Blondie and Talking Heads). All I had was an early demo, but on the back of that I did a deal with him to sign to his Radioactive label (via MCA in the US) and he introduced me to producer Danny Saber. Danny's input was essential for how I wanted the first Black Grape album to sound, but some of the bigwigs at MCA were a little nervous about handing over all the responsibility for the whole album to Danny alone, because he came from a hip-hop background. So they brought in Stephen Lironi, from Altered Images, who was married to Clare Grogan, as a more traditional pop producer to watch over Danny, but we all worked great together. Recording *It's Great When You're Straight... Yeah* was a blast.

Working with Kurfirst was great. I mean, it was just great to have someone believe in me, after all the shit that I'd been through with the collapse of Factory and the Mondays. It was my first taste of being A&R'd. I'd never really been A&R'd before, Factory didn't really do that sort of thing. Usually the A&R guy who signs a band to a record label would then be the one who oversees their recording and is the one who agrees with the band on what records to put out, or sometimes will advise on what direction he thinks the band should be going. Maybe he would come down to the studio and have a listen during recording and chuck his twopenneth in, whether the band like it or not. That sort of thing didn't happen with Factory. They just let you get on with it. They usually didn't even ask to hear anything when we were recording, or check we actually had any songs before they booked an expensive studio for us. They usually didn't hear anything until we'd finished the album, and we'd give it to them and say, 'Here y'are, it's done.'

With Black Grape I was really confident we'd done something good, but I don't think some of the label heads were convinced the album would sell by the truckload. We'd given them stuff with a lot of hip-hop influence like 'Reverend Black Grape' and 'A Big Day In The North', and Kurfirst said, 'Look, I need something a bit more white and rock'n'roll from you.' We went back and ended up putting a big guitar lick on 'Kelly's Heroes' to appease them. Which sounded great, but I still preferred the original version when it was a bit more hip-hop. But we had to compromise a bit. I don't think either Kurfirst or the label were sure where to put us when they first heard the record. Obviously Britpop was everywhere in 1995, and there wasn't really anything that sounded like Black Grape back then. You certainly didn't have any other bands with a white guy trying to do rocky, hip-hop-influenced stuff like ours, apart from maybe Beastie Boys. But I knew it would work, and it did.

Looking back on everything that happened when Factory went down, I'm fine with it now, after all this time. To be fair, I don't think Tony ever really blamed us at the time. I think Tony knew he'd fucked up. He gave an interview to the *NME* just after Factory had gone down, and they asked him if he would do it all again given the chance, and he said, 'Yes, of course I'd do it all again, provided I had the groups. You can always deal with the business side, but you have to have the groups. If you don't have great music, forget it. I'd do it all again because of the opportunity to work with Ian Curtis and Shaun Ryder.'

# Live gigs

A lot of people think that the bigger the gig, the more nerve-wracking it must be, especially when you get to headlining Glastonbury or playing Wembley or stadium gigs. But I've done all of those and, to be honest, I always found the smaller gigs much harder. The bigger the gigs got, the easier I found it. I'm more at ease playing Wembley than a really intimate venue to a hundred people. Let me explain...

When we first started Happy Mondays, I really wasn't arsed about playing live. I was happy jamming with my mates and coming up with songs, but the rest of the band really wanted to start playing live. The first ever gig we did was at the youth club at Wardley Community Centre, which is in Swinton in Salford, near my gran's old house. I can actually remember that gig better than I can headlining Glastonbury or some of the huge headline gigs we did later on. I remember Paul Davies, who had joined as keyboard player but wasn't ready to play live yet, coming back and saying there were girls hanging out waiting for us. Our first gig and girls wanted to chat to us, that's when I first thought there could be some benefits to playing live. The gig felt like it was pretty rammed, but it was only a small room so there were probably only about twenty-five or thirty people there. No one who was there that night went on to form a band.

For the first couple of years I found it quite hard because we were playing really small venues. Sometimes there wouldn't even be a stage, so I'd be on the same level as the audience and could see the whites of their eyes. Being a bit of a geezer, I just found it really fucking ridiculous to try and wiggle my hips and be rock'n'roll when I'm nose to nose with blokes stood a foot away from me. I just felt a bit of a lemon. It's tough, it's hard work, and that's when you learn your craft.

It's not that I don't like small gigs, I just find them difficult. Places like the Adelphi in Hull, which is basically just a terraced house converted into a venue, and you're playing to a hundred people. Or Corbieres in Manchester, which was a tiny basement bar on Half Moon Street, just off St Ann's Square and held about 150 people. I totally get that those gigs are exciting, seeing a band that you're into in a small, sweaty venue. People remember those gigs, like The Beatles at the Cavern, but I just find it hard work to try and be a rock star when you're literally toe to toe with someone who's standing there with his pint, just staring at you. People in Manchester still talk about our early gig in Corbieres as some seminal underground gig, and I probably would have loved it if I was there in the audience, but on stage I felt too self-conscious because half the audience were my mates and they're basically stood right next to you. I say 'on stage' but there wasn't even a stage. We were basically playing in the corner of the room on the floor, so we were at the same eye level as the audience. I just felt ridiculous.

Ask any band, those small early gigs are tough. When Oasis were starting out, they would be bottom of the bill at the Boardwalk, playing to about twenty people. It's a rainy Monday night and they're playing to a handful of people, most of whom are waiting to see their mates who are in the next band, and Liam is standing there singing to them, 'Toonnniiiight, I'm a rock'n'roll star'. Noel said lads were sniggering behind their hands, smirking, 'Yeah, course you are, mate!' But they believed it, and they were proved right, and that same lad who was smirking at Liam was probably desperately trying to get tickets to see them play at Maine Road two years later, telling all his pals how he was there at the start and always knew they were going to be big.

Noel tells a story about how Oasis played the Duchess of York in Leeds in their early days, and nobody turned up. Literally nobody. Not one fucking person. But Oasis just thought 'Fuck it' and they played the gig anyway to an empty room. In between the songs it was so quiet all you could hear was the barman wiping glasses. Next thing, the band take off and Oasis become an overnight success, and a few months later they're back playing the same venue and there's queues around the block. Absolutely rammed. Halfway through the gig, Liam announces: 'This one's for everyone who came last time we played here!' and people in the crowd cheered as if they were there. Noel was like, 'You lying Yorkshire bastards!'

What's that saying? Success has many fathers. Yeah, and they all reckon they were at your early gigs.

When we first start playing live, I also didn't really like people concentrating on me as the focal point of attention, which is slightly unusual for a front man and the opposite of someone like Bono, who's only happy when he's the focus of attention. I was big and boisterous off stage – I'd be the life and soul of the party if I was down the pub with my mates – but when I got on stage I used to shrink a bit. There's a cliché that front men 'come alive' when they go on stage, but in those early days I was the fucking opposite. I was full of it off stage, but then would shrink a bit when it was showtime.

There were a couple of bands we were lucky enough to play with early on that we learned a lot from. New Order took us out on tour really early on, because we were signed to Factory like them, and that was a big learning curve. That was our first time playing bigger venues, and for the first time it felt real and I thought, 'I can do this.' New Order were also great because they didn't give a fuck. They played the gig the way they wanted and didn't even bother doing an encore.

It was also good for us because one of their sound guys, Eddie, did our sound for us, so we sounded much better on stage. Bernard was quite into us. I think he liked the fact that we didn't sound like anyone else, but also the fact that we came from a working-class background in Salford, like him and Hooky. Almost everyone else associated with Factory – from Tony Wilson to Vini Reilly, and most of other bands – were middle-class, so I think Bernard found it a breath of fresh air to have someone from the same background on the label. Hooky was more wary of us, though. He still treated us as a bunch of scallies who would probably rob them blind given half a chance.

The other band who took us on tour as support was The Colourfield, which was Terry Hall's band after The Specials and Fun Boy Three. I think that came about because Mike Pickering was mates with Terry Hall, even though Mike is a big City fan and Terry's a big United fan. Terry's from Coventry but he was living in Manchester at the time. I was a big fan of The Specials, but also Fun Boy Three and The Colourfield. Terry Hall was a brilliant front man. Observing Terry play live up close was a real eye-opener for me because he was such a quiet guy off stage. He'd hardly say a word or look you in the eye, but then he got on stage and was really confident and confrontational, engaging with the audience and calling people out. It really showed me a different way of being a front man. A lot of people thought Terry was not arsed and didn't care, but that wasn't the case at all. He really knew how to work a crowd, but in a different way. It was the first time I'd seen a different kind of front man at work – someone who wasn't showing off and shouting 'look at me'. That helped me a lot and, looking back, probably gave me more confidence that I could do it, because even at that stage I definitely knew I wasn't the type to be at the front of the stage, milking the audience's attention like a lot of front men do. But Terry showed me that you didn't have to go down that route, there was another way to be a front man.

Because we'd signed to Factory quite early on, we were still learning the ropes and we had to do our growing up as a band in public really. We didn't even know how a band rehearsed properly, we'd just developed our own way of jamming and doing things. So I once went along to see The Colourfield rehearse in Liverpool, just to see how they did it, and even that was an eye-opener as I'd never seen another band rehearse before.

When we first went to London for gigs we'd all travel down in a Transit. The first London show we did was in Hammersmith at the Clarendon, playing with The Weather Prophets and Pop Will Eat Itself. Jeff Barrett put that gig on. He was a big fan of the band and he was one of the first people to get the Mondays in London, and he ended up really helping the band. He was working with Alan McGee at Creation at the time, and doing gigs on the side, but then he ended up setting up his own press company and doing our press. Both Jeff and Alan were big fans of Factory, so they were on our side and on the same page. Mind you, the first time we met Jeff, he thought we were a bunch of drunks off the street. There was a big Irish boozer next to the venue and, the way he remembers it, he came in and saw a big bunch of blokes slumped against the wall with dozens of tins of lager and bottles of cider. He thought we were just a bunch of Irish drunks, so he came over and asked us to move outside, and we were like, 'But we're playing tonight, we're Happy Mondays.' He couldn't believe it. He loved it. He'd never seen a band like us.

We had brought one of New Order's sound guys Oz down with us, and he got a great sound, and that was a bit of a turning point for us, as it got people like Jeff and some of the London music press that were there on our side. They got to see what we were really like and how different we were and we started to get decent write-ups after that. It wasn't long after that *Melody Maker* said that our next single, 'Freaky Dancin'', was single of the week and they called it 'the best single of the year so far'.

We got different reactions at those early gigs because people had really seen nothing like us. We did a gig at King George's Hall in Blackburn with The Railway Children, which turned into a riot. There was fighting between lads from Blackburn and Manchester in the audience and some kid got on stage and started shouting 'Blackburn Youth, Blackburn Youth,' so Bez just smacked him in the mouth and it all went off. The audience were chucking pint pots and one hit our keyboard player, PD, in the head, and Bez smacked the lad in the face and was then hitting him on the head with his maracas.

There were two main things that helped get me over that nervousness on stage. One was we started to play bigger venues, where I found it much easier with a slight distance between you and the crowd. It feels like a proper gig then, and you don't feel ridiculous behaving like a singer or being more rock'n'roll, like you would do when you're only performing in front of thirty people. Once you're playing to 5000 people or 10,000 people, or stadiums, it doesn't feel real. Instead of seeing individual reactions in people's eyes, you just see a sea of faces, and I was far more comfortable with that. The second thing that helped me get over it was, let's be honest, drink and drugs. I don't think I went on stage straight for about twenty-five years.

Because we took off pretty quickly, the Mondays jumped those mid-sized venues first time around. We jumped straight from playing a few hundred to G-Mex and Wembley Arena,

10,000-capacity shows. We never played Manchester Apollo and Brixton Academy first time around. We missed them out and went straight to the huge venues. It was only with Black Grape that I went back and played those mid-size venues like the Apollo and Brixton.

You'd be surprised how many of those legendary venues are pretty basic backstage. The Apollo and Brixton haven't changed for years and you have to go up and down these winding brick staircases to get on stage. They're not the only ones, though. Whisky a Go Go on Sunset Boulevard in Los Angeles or CBGB in New York – most of those sorts of places that are legendary venues in your mind, when you get there, the reality is they're shitholes. It's like playing in the tap room or the vault at your local Holts boozer in Salford.

Nowadays, gigs and touring has become one of a band's most important incomes, since record sales fell off a cliff with everyone streaming and downloading everything for free. But we were ahead of the game on that score. We always knew you could make decent money for gigs. Before the Mondays first took off, we had been playing venues that held a few hundred, and the Haçienda, but when it happened we knew we had the fanbase to go straight to the big gaffs. Usually, the next step up for a band would have been mid-sized venues that hold about 3000 or 4000, but we knew we were riding a wave of something, so we wanted to do G-Mex, which holds 10,000. Simon Moran, who runs SJM concerts who are now the biggest and best concert promoters in the country – they put on Oasis at Knebworth – was still just starting out then, and he got nervous about it. He thought it was too risky. So we thought, 'Fuck it, we'll do it ourselves,' and got a pal of ours to promote it for us. We put it on sale, and within a couple of days, he was like, 'This is happening, tickets are flying, we should put another night on sale,' and before you knew it, we'd shifted 20,000 tickets.

You get some gigs that are big moments for you, but you don't always treat them as such. G-Mex we knew was a big thing and that felt like a moment. When we headlined Glastonbury, we just sort of turned up and did it. You watch it now and see how much effort Jay-Z or Stormzy or someone puts into their set. Months and months of planning and choreography. We just turned up and did it. When we played Rock in Rio, which is the biggest gig I've ever played, we had been off our boxes enjoying Rio for five days before and we just turned up and did the gig, in a thunderstorm. When we did our first gig in New York we blew it a bit, as I mentioned before, but what do you expect? Oasis did the same thing, ended up on crystal meth and were up all night and missed their gig. They all got the wrong set list and started playing different songs, which is arguably even worse than us!

# Riders

When you're on tour you usually get given a rider each night at the gig. When you're just starting out you don't get much and you don't get any choice. If you're the support band you can be lucky to get anything. Maybe the venue or the headline act will leave you a crate of lager or something. A couple of plates of sandwiches if you're lucky. It's when you make it and you're headlining your own tours that you can actually request your own rider. It gets included in the contract when the band gets booked. Along with the fee you're getting, the production you expect at the venue, and all that technical stuff, there will be a rider, which details what food and drink and whatever else the band demands, and it's up to the promoter and the gig venue to provide it and pay for it.

Some musicians' riders can be a hundred fucking pages long. Van Halen's rider famously demanded they had a bowl of M&Ms with all the brown ones taken out. Although they later claimed they only put that in there to check that people were reading it. Madonna has a 200-strong entourage, and she takes her own furniture everywhere so her dressing room looks like her house. No wonder she needs 200 people in her entourage if she's moving bloody house every night! Paul McCartney has famously been veggie for years, so his rider demands there's no fur, leather or meat in his dressing room, right down to no leather seats in his limousine or whatever cars they're suppling for the gig. Mary J. Blige hates sharing a toilet – she has a bit of a phobia about it – so she demands a private toilet with a brand-new toilet seat wherever she plays a gig. Since he went clean, Eminem demands a set of weights in his dressing room so he can work out. Jack White from the White Stripes has a rider that says 'NO BANANA TOUR', as apparently someone in his band is dead allergic to bananas. Grace Jones is quite demanding, which is no surprise. Her rider is very specific about exactly what vintage champagne she demands, down to what year it is and everything, plus details on what oysters and sushi she likes, and how they should be prepared. Cher's rider even includes a dedicated 'wig' room. I don't think the Mondays will be requesting one of those soon!

When the Rolling Stones are on tour it's like a huge travelling circus, and there's a whole suite of different rooms and dressing rooms backstage. Keith even used to have his own English pub built backstage every night. They have their own chefs who prepare their food every day, which includes a shepherd's pie each night for Keith Richards. No one is allowed to break the crust of the shepherd's pie apart from Keith – that's a big no-no. They brought in that strict rule after someone ate Keith's shepherd's pie before a gig in Toronto once and he refused to go on stage until the catering staff had made him another one. Jagger was furious apparently, so they brought in the shepherd's pie rule to make sure it didn't happen again. The rest of the band and their entourage are allowed to have some of it, but *only* after Keith has broken the crust. No one's allowed to go near it until then! Keith even talked about it in his autobiography, *Life*: 'It's now famous, my rule on the road. Nobody touches the shepherd's pie till I've been there. Don't bust my crust, baby.'

The first proper tour we went on, we were supporting New Order and we didn't get a rider, which we really could have done with as we were all fucking skint at the time. When we played the Haçienda with them, I was starving and they had a rider and we didn't. Instead of waiting till no one was watching, and nicking something, I thought, 'I'll be polite here,' and asked if I could get a drink and a sandwich from their rider. Hooky said, 'No... no, you can't.' I thought, 'If you weren't in New Order I'd poke your eye out, you cheeky bastard.' I know Hooky well now and he'd be the first to admit he didn't like us initially.

I've never had a pre-gig routine. You hear about all these singers that gargle with lemon and honey or whatever, but I never used to bother. My pre-gig routine for a long time was heroin. Simple as that. As long as I had my heroin fix, I was fine to go on. Funnily enough, out of all the Mondays, it was Bez who was the most fixated about his pre-gig routine. He used to have all these vitamin tablets and supplements, and all these energy drinks. But then he'd wash that all down with his ecstasy. I could never get my head round it. He was always insisting that he needed all these supplements and energy drinks to keep up his energy to dance on stage, as if they were the tools of his trade or something… but then he'd go and neck five Es. I'd be like, 'Fucking hell, Bez. I think you might find it's the five Es that are keeping you dancing all night, mate, not all these daft energy drinks we're paying for!'

When the band first took off, we had these caterers on tour with us preparing great food, but it was a bit of a waste, really. Half the time we didn't want to eat anything if we were off our heads. Even when we were hungry, we just wanted simple food. We were young lads, and all we wanted was Holland pies, chips and beans. I used to have chips for tea almost every night when I was growing up for a while, as my mam and dad ran a chippy. I can still remember the smell of the freshly baked pies being delivered at six o'clock in the morning. It was actually a good chippy, and my mam and dad were a bit more forward-thinking than most, because they served curry sauce, which not many places did back then, not in Salford anyway.

The Mondays even had three tour buses at one stage. One for the band, one for the roadies, and one for catering. God knows how much that cost us. We could have just sent someone out to the chippy and saved us a fortune!

# *Top of the Pops*

It's hard for kids nowadays to appreciate just how huge *Top of the Pops* was back in the day. My youngest kids have grown up with YouTube and social media and they can watch their favourite singers and bands anytime they want at the touch of a button. When I was a kid, the only time you saw bands on TV was Thursday nights on *Top of the Pops*. It was the first time you got to see what bands looked like. I try saying to my kids, 'Imagine if YouTube was only on for half an hour, once a week, on Thursday night, and you couldn't even choose what video you wanted, you had to wait to see what bands came on.' That really is impossible for kids nowadays to get their head around. But that's how much *Top of the Pops* meant, and it used to get nearly 20 million people watching it. That's a third of the country! Next day at school, everyone would be saying, 'Fucking hell, did you see Bowie on *Top of the Pops* last night?!'

To put it in perspective, the big Saturday-night TV show

that's on at the moment, *The Masked Singer*, was in the news one week because it got 8.9 million viewers and they were talking about how that was a 'phenomenon'. Back in our day, *Top of the Pops* used to get more than double that every week! And that was early evening on a Thursday, not prime-time Saturday night.

I remember seeing the Small Faces on there when I was only six or seven, and thinking, 'Wow, they look smart, they look cool.' Then, about three years later, my other strong memory of *Top of the Pops* as a kid was watching David Bowie as Ziggy Stardust in 1972, singing 'Star Man' with his electric-blue guitar. I can remember that really clearly because Bowie looked cool as fuck. Later on, I remember The Clash and New Order refusing to mime on *Top of the Pops*, and thinking that was cool, although I changed my mind about miming much later, after I'd been through the experience myself.

When it first launched, *Top of the Pops* was actually filmed in Manchester, although I didn't know that when I was a kid. The first *Top of the Pops* was on New Year's Day 1964, filmed in an old converted church in Rusholme in Manchester. The Stones were the first band on, with 'I Wanna Be Your Man', and Dusty Springfield was on as well. It was presented by Jimmy Savile, although everyone would rather forget that now. They continued filming *Top of the Pops* in Manchester for the first couple of years, before they moved it to London. George Best was even dancing in the audience for one of the first shows, watching the Stones, before he became known as 'El Beatle'.

Growing up, as far as I was concerned, if someone made it onto *Top of the Pops* they were famous. They were a pop star and they were made for life. It was seeing the Faces and Bowie on *Top of the Pops* that first made me think how cool it would be to be in a band.

The first time we did *Top of the Pops* was in 1989 for 'Hallelujah' from our *Madchester Rave On* EP. Tony Wilson had been desperate for us to get a single in the charts and Factory had brought in Steve Lillywhite to produce the single. He was married to Kirsty MacColl at the time, and she was a fan of ours, so she came in and did backing vocals on 'Hallelujah'. I thought Kirsty was great, and she ended up hanging out with us a bit and did a few gigs, and we asked her to join us on *Top of the Pops*. She'd already done the show a few times, on her own and with The Pogues for 'The Fairytale of New York'. In fact, she'd been on it again only a few months before she did it with us, with her cover of 'Days' by The Kinks.

What made our first *Top of the Pops* even more memorable was The Stone Roses were also on the same show, so it felt like Manchester and this new scene was taking over, and we were the figureheads of that. Loads of people still remember that as a big moment. I still get blokes in their fifties coming up to me now, saying, 'I was at college when you and the Roses were on *Top of the Pops* and it was fucking brilliant!' Even Dom Joly, when we were in the jungle doing *I'm A Celebrity… Get Me Out Of Here!*, was banging on about watching it with his pals at uni.

We shared a dressing room with the Roses, and me and Ian Brown had to have our make-up done at the same time. He remembers me asking if I could have his make-up, 'He's a good-looking fucker – look at my big hooter! Give me his make-up!'

Because a lot of the wider general public didn't really know what we looked like, I thought it would be funny to mix it up a bit. I wanted Ian to front the Mondays, me to play bass in the Roses, Mani to play the drums with the Mondays and so on, just all swap over and mix it up. It would have been really funny because only fans of the Mondays and Roses would have noticed and got the joke. But because it was the first time we'd all been on *Top of the Pops*, the rest of them weren't really up for it. Maybe they were thinking this might be the only chance we'll get to be on *Top of the Pops* so they wanted to make the most of it, they wanted something to show their grandkids in fifty years. Only Bez was up for it in the end, so we sacked it off.

I had a bit of a run-in with the bloke who was running the *Top of the Pops* studio that day. What a dick. I wasn't even really misbehaving. He was just a pompous arse, a stuck-up TV type who tried ordering me about and I just said, 'Fuck off, knobhead.' He was giving it all, '*I'm* the boss, I'm in charge here!' and I said, 'I don't give a fuck who you are, you silly little cunt.'

'*You* will *never* do *Top of the Pops* again.'

'Fuck off, you dick.'

Funny thing was, by the time I went back to do it again, which was less than six months later, he was the one that had been fired. I ended up doing *Top of the Pops* numerous times with the Mondays and Black Grape, and I even presented it in 1996.

The other thing I remember from our first *Top of the Pops* performance was our guitarist, Mark Day, was still a postman and had to get back to Manchester that night so he could do his fucking post round the next morning! Poor Mark never saw rock'n'roll as a great prospect. He's a brilliant guitarist but was never cut out to be rock'n'roll – he's just too square. He was always complaining, in his dopey cow voice, that 'Rock'n'roll's not a proper job. You don't get a pension with it.' That's the *whole point*, you prick! That's why you get into rock'n'roll. Because you don't want a proper job. You don't get into rock'n'roll if you're worried about your fucking final-salary pension!

All our mates were made up for us being on *Top of the Pops*. They thought it was great. The only people who had an issue with it were bloody student types, saying, 'I'm not into the Mondays any more now they've been on *Top of the Pops*.' Dickheads. People like that used to wind me up. If I was into a band when I was a kid, I would have loved it if they had made it onto *Top of the Pops*. The last thing I would have thought was they'd sold out. You've got to remember that there was no one else like us on *Top of the Pops*, the whole charts had gone squeaky clean and pop, like Bros and all these Stock Aitken Waterman acts. If I was a kid sat at home watching *Top of the Pops* and the Mondays and Roses came on, I would have been buzzing that at last someone who looked like me had made it on there, and I know kids felt like that because they still come up and mention it to me now. There's always been a weird bit of Britain's psyche, where they build you up to knock you down, and with music there's also that indie mentality with some people where they want to keep you to themselves. If they're into the band they want it to be their little secret, and they don't want them getting big and popular and other people getting in on it. Well, sorry mate, we always wanted to be big and on *Top of the Pops*, and I won't apologize for that. Who wants to keep playing little basement gigs to the same hundred people all their life?

You did have the odd friend or family member who found it odd that this kid from Salford they'd known all their life was now on *Top of the Pops*. 808 State made it to *Top of the Pops* about the same time as us, with 'Pacific State', and Andy and Darren from the band were still working as roofers at the time. When they came back home after filming the show in London, Andy said his mam couldn't believe it. She was laughing at him, saying, 'What are *you lot* doing on *Top of the Pops*?!'

After that first time we appeared on *Top of the Pops*, everything just seemed to step up another level. We would get recognized everywhere, and I felt like everyone wanted a piece of me. Suddenly everyone wanted a piece of Manchester. Everyone from *Blue Peter* to *Panorama* to Japanese TV crews descended on Manchester and it was usually me and Bez they wanted to speak to. The requests for interviews didn't stop. I was on the front cover of the *NME* again, this time me and Tony Wilson, photographed outside Factory's new offices, with the headline 'Manchester so much to answer for'. Wilson was being typical Wilson, revelling in it: 'My psychiatrist asked me whether my immaturity bothers me. I told him in this industry it was an asset.' Wilson spent the interview comparing Madchester to everything from the death of Thatcherism to the fall of the Berlin Wall. I was never one to make big statements like that. I just said, 'Wilson goes over the top, always has done. This is real for us, it's our way out.'

The second time we were on was for 'Step On', in March 1990, which was another step up for us, and ended up getting to No.5 in the charts. Back when getting in the Top 10 actually meant something. Rowetta had joined us by then, so she was on *Top of the Pops* with us. It really felt like we had become established by then. Even Mark Day thought so, because he finally quit his job as a postie! Our manager Nathan McGough had upped our wages to £150 a week, which was about the same as Mark was getting from the Post Office, and we were about to do our biggest ever headline gigs, at G-Mex in Manchester and Wembley Arena in London, so Mark finally felt secure enough to stop doing his morning round!

We spent that summer recording *Pills 'n' Thrills and Bellyaches* in Los Angeles, then we were back on *Top of the Pops* again for the lead single from that album, 'Kinky Afro', which also went to No.5. I'd just got a bowlcut haircut and I look like I'm smirking a bit behind my fringe if you look back at it now.

Then in early 1991, we were back on there again, with 'Loose Fit', which was our fourth appearance on *Top of the Pops* in just fourteen months. A lot had happened in that short time, and I think you can tell from our body language that we were all a bit fucked. I was, certainly. I felt like everyone wanted a piece of me, with the endless interviews and gigs, plus the effects of my drug habit, and being a new dad. I was knackered and badly needed a break. From being really excited about first doing *Top of the Pops* a little over a year earlier, it had quickly got to the stage where they had to gee me up to get me on stage, and use make-up to cover the bags under my eyes.

When I went back and did *Top of the Pops* with Black Grape, for 'Reverend Black Grape', I thought I was going to be censored. I was in rehearsals in the afternoon when it came to the line 'Go put your Reeboks on, man/And go play fucking tennis', I kept expecting them to say, 'Look, you're going to have to change this. You can't say "fucking" on *Top of the Pops*,' but they never did. Somehow they didn't get on it. They must have presumed I said 'funky tennis' or something.

I did get banned from Channel 4 shortly after that though, for swearing too much. I thought it was a bit over the top myself, but it didn't bother me. I didn't give a fuck at that age. I also knew that people would lap that up. Look at the Sex Pistols – hardly anyone had heard of them before they went on the *Today* programme and swore at Bill Grundy, and they made the front page of the next day's *Daily Mirror*. That's what basically brought punk to the attention of the mainstream. That probably changed the face of British music history. They couldn't get arrested before then. Apparently, Queen were supposed to be the guests on the show that week but they couldn't do it, so Eric Hall, who later went on to be a famous show-business and football agent and manage East 17 but was working at EMI at the time, persuaded the *Today* programme to have the Pistols on instead.

There's a clip filmed backstage at *Top of the Pops* on the Black Grape documentary *Grape Tapes*. It's me making a chart run-down of my favourite drugs: 'And at No.4 this week, two bags of heroin, down three places from last week…' Not my finest moment, I admit.

They do all the re-runs of *Top of the Pops* now on BBC4, and I quite enjoy it when I catch a bit of it. I'm not generally one for nostalgia, and everything has to move on, but nothing's ever replaced *Top of the Pops* really.

# Drugs

People are always going to associate Shaun Ryder and
the Mondays and Black Grape with drugs. Because
people love those stories of debauchery, and those
stories have stuck. Although it's fair to say there is no smoke
without fire. I've been pretty open about the fact that I had
a long relationship with drugs, particularly heroin. We also
did a fair bit of dealing in the early years of the band. We
needed to at the time, as we weren't making enough from
the band to live on. We started the band in 1982 and didn't
make a living out of it until we took off in 1989, so we had
to find another way to survive.

Drugs had always been around, since I was a teenager.
There was a lot of speed, weed and heroin around when I
was growing up, and we dabbled in a bit of everything. Like
Noel Gallagher said, the middle classes experiment with
drugs, but the working classes just get stuck in. There's also
that Mick Jagger quote, 'You start out playing rock'n'roll

so you can have sex and do drugs, but you end up doing drugs so you can still play rock'n'roll and have sex.' Speak for yourself, mate.

I first dabbled in heroin in 1982. When you first do it, you love it or hate it, and when I first smoked it I instantly got this Ready Brek glow – an 'I don't give a fuck' feeling. I was really wary about getting sucked in, though. It wasn't until the band started to take off that I really got a habit. It was partly because it calmed my nerves before going on stage and, before I knew it, I was smoking it every day.

In the mid-eighties, there was a time when me and Bez took acid every day for a good year. *Every day*. It got to the stage where we were eating black microdots, which are quite strong acid, and they didn't even phase us any more. I never had a really bad trip. I think you can bring bad trips on yourself. I've got a pretty strong mind, so even when it was incredibly powerful acid and the real world disappeared and I was submerged in a complete cartoon existence, I was always able to say to myself, 'This is a trip.' I always, *always* had a strong enough mind to know what was happening. Even when the world was one big cartoon and I looked up at the clouds and they'd turned into great big Greek gods, climbing down out of the sky and talking to me – even then, I always had a strong enough mind, as did Bez, to say, 'No, this is just a trip, don't freak out.' The only time I remember really getting into a state on acid, was when me and Bez watched *Watership Down* on a trip one day. We couldn't handle it – both of us ended up crying, in bits.

I suppose I should mention again the infamous story about me and Bez trying crack cocaine on our first trip to

New York. We'd heard about crack before we got to New York and were determined to try it because you couldn't get it back home at the time. When you're looking for drugs, you generally know the score – you can weigh up the situation and tell who's dealing and what's what. You only have to look at the right person a certain way and you'll clock each other, and you've done the deal without even saying any words, just by eyeballs and movements. We met this geezer on the street and got chatting to him and he told us he'd been in Vietnam, and he knew what we were after so he said, 'Come to my crib, man.' So we went to his crib, which was in the basement of a nearby building. He built the pipe for us and I went first. Bez was going, 'What's it like? What's it like? What's it like?' and I just went, 'Fuuucckin hell… fuuuuuccckkkininnnnnnn hhhhhheelllllll… I'm going through fucking space,' and Bez was like, 'Lemme have a go! LEMME HAVE A GO!'

But it was ecstasy that changed everything, for me and the band. Musically, financially, mentally, socially. That was when everything went from black and white to technicolour, and we rode the buzz and the wave. When Es first arrived, we were the first to get them, and we were knocking them out at £25. Most nights we were making more money than the club itself. Bez was a terrible drug dealer. A nightmare. He's great at getting the word out, but a terrible businessman. The worst. A dealer's mantra is don't get high on your own supply, but no one told Bez that. I'm not saying I didn't dip in myself – I'm no saint obviously – but Bez was the worst. If he had twenty Es to sell, he'd take four himself and then end up giving the rest away.

Ecstasy affected everything. I remember one incident with

a load of squaddies in Driffield in Yorkshire, while we were there recording *Bummed*, our second album. Driffield really is a funny old place and the Mondays and our crew stuck out like a sore thumb, really. There was only one little disco in town, but a big army base. We went to the one club one Friday night and it was full of squaddies on a night off. Before E, if all our lot were just on the beer, it would probably have kicked off *big* time quite quickly, because the lads that I was with wouldn't have backed down. But that night we were all on ecstasy. One of the squaddies had a problem with Bez and because I was on E I tried to be the peacekeeper: 'Listen, he's just off his head.' As I was chatting to the squaddie I just said, 'Look, get one of these down you. It will change your life, and you'll know what we're on about,' and gave him an E. He was really drunk and just took it. Twenty minutes later he was a changed man. He came bouncing over to us, 'Wowwwww! This is amazing! Gimme some more for my mates!' They ended up buying some off us, and pretty soon all these squaddies were sweating and hugging each other, off their faces, saying 'I don't want to go back fighting wars, man!' Hilarious. We couldn't stop laughing.

The drugs changed after the initial acid house explosion in Manchester and it got a bit dark, as cocaine and heroin came back in and the gangs moved in. As I mentioned earlier, I was back on the heroin after we started Black Grape. The title of the debut album *It's Great When You're Straight… Yeah* was a bit of a joke. I don't think we were straight for the first two years of Black Grape.

It wasn't just heroin with Black Grape, though. There was a huge cocktail of drugs flying about at that time. All sorts. Cocaine, heroin, weed, ecstasy. For a little while our favourite drug was temazepam. I can't even remember who first suggested it or how we got into it. It's a wild, mad drug. You can never remember a thing afterwards because that's what it's supposed to do – to make you forget about stuff. They use it for soldiers to cope with PTSD after wars and stuff like that. It's not designed to be used as a cocktail by Mancunian pop stars with cocaine, alcohol and whatever else. I even wrote a song called 'Tramazi Party' about the experience and the mad nights we would have at that time while we were on it. I remember waking up in the basement of a restaurant one time, naked, with two naked waitresses and not having the faintest clue where I was or how I ended up there. I also had a gun on me and there were three bullets missing from the chamber. Twenty-five years later I still haven't got a fucking clue what happened that night. We'd do mad things like rent a gaff in the woods in the middle of nowhere and have a tramazi party and it would all go west and nobody could tell what anybody else was saying. I'd get up in the morning and there would be all these bodies lying around on the floor, all these people totally fucked.

One silver lining with drugs for me is that they prevented alcohol from really getting a grip of me. Alcohol in a lot of ways can do more long-lasting damage than drugs. Look at people like Keith Moon, and Bon Scott from AC/DC who died early from alcohol abuse. You don't have to be a rock star to suffer the long-term effects of alcohol. They've clamped down on smoking now and you can't smoke anywhere, but alcohol is still never frowned upon. Even after lockdown was lifted, they wanted to encourage everyone to get down the pub. Probably because they're raking it on alcohol duty.

Why do I think I took so many drugs back in the day? There's no one reason. Part of it is the rock'n'roll lifestyle, it's what I bought into from day one – even before day one, from when I was an eleven-year-old bunking off school and watching *Stardust*. Sex, drugs and rock'n'roll, that was what I was sold on. But, as I said earlier, the sex and drugs came before the rock'n'roll. I was doing drugs, even hard drugs, before the band started. There was a lot of them about in Salford and Manchester when we were growing up. I also took them because they were great, a lot of the time. Until they weren't. When you get in a band, you use drink and drugs as a crutch to help you cope with everything. It's a mental life to lead, really. It's not real, so being on drugs can take the edge off it. Also, back then I had a lot of self-doubt – I think all the band did – and so I used drugs to help mask that.

I don't party like I used to. I haven't for quite a while. It's nearly twenty years now since I cleaned up my act. I knew once I got to my forties that things had to change. If you're going as hard at it when you're nearly fifty as you were when you were twenty, then you're in trouble and there's something a bit sad about you. Plenty of people still think I cane it all the time. I still get people coming up to me in Asda or TK Maxx, offering me a line, for fuck's sake. I'm nearly sixty, mate, and you really think I want to do a line in TK Maxx on a Tuesday afternoon?! Sometimes I'll just laugh, sometimes it winds me up, it just depends what mood I'm in.

# Rehab

I've been in rehab a few times. When they tried to make me go to rehab, I didn't say 'no, no, no'. I didn't put up much of a fight, to be honest. When Factory first suggested it to me, part of me thought, 'Here we go, another rock and roll cliché.' I didn't put up much resistance and I agreed to it, but the first couple of times I went in it was a bit pointless because I wasn't ready. You have to be ready to do it, and motivated, or there's not much point.

I think half the time when musicians end up in rehab, it's obviously due to drugs and alcohol, but it's also a combination of the pressure and lifestyle that have driven them to rely on the drink or drugs. Plus the fact that everywhere you go as a successful musician, people are offering you free drink and drugs. No one bats an eyelid at someone doing something to excess in the music industry as it's so widespread. I'm not just talking about musicians, I'm talking about the whole music industry, from A&Rs to radio pluggers. Someone will disappear for a bit, for a few weeks, to 'take a bit of time out' and quite often that means they've been in rehab.

A few musicians will take the piss a bit when other musicians go into rehab, but I think generally they're supportive if they know someone has issues. Apparently, Keith Richards was one of the ones persuading Ronnie Wood to go into rehab, but when Ronnie checked himself in, there was a bunch of flowers waiting for him from Keith with a card that just said 'You lightweight, love Keith'. Alan McGee, who's now my manager, has also been through rehab and is quite open about it. 'We all took too many drugs, and I accept that my behaviour was quite mad,' he admits. He signed Oasis and then missed a lot of their rise to stardom as he was taking time out to get clean. Primal Scream were at their most debauched at the time and called him a lightweight but, like I say, I think people are more understanding nowadays. Bobby Gillespie from the Primals has now been clean for a few years and he said a couple of years ago, in an interview with *Huck* magazine:

> We just did what we did and never really thought about the consequences. I think when you're young you feel immortal. As I got older, and I was still using drugs, and I began to have children…
>
> I mean, I was putting myself through hell. I wasn't having a good time. When I was younger, I just thought that's the price you pay for being high. At first, it's kind of glamorous and exciting – 'Look! I'm Lou Reed, I'm Iggy!' – but as you get older, it's not a dignified thing to

be involved in. You can't get out of bed for two days, you hate yourself, you did embarrassing things, said embarrassing things. It's like you're haunted. Drug addiction is a possession. The longer it goes on, the more extreme the behaviour and the self-loathing.

I agree with him about not really thinking about the consequences when you're younger. That's why I wasn't ready for rehab back then. The first time I went into rehab was when the Mondays were first taking off, and we'd just done *Top of the Pops* and I'd realized I was famous. I'd been using heroin more and more over the previous year, but I still didn't see it as much of a problem. It was our manager Nathan McGough and Factory who persuaded me to do rehab, and I agreed to go to The Priory in Altrincham, just outside Manchester. I'm sure part of the thinking behind it was that the Mondays were just starting to make money for the first time, and they didn't want my habit to derail the whole Mondays gravy train. But I wasn't ready for it at all, and it was a waste of time. A waste of everybody's time and money. I'd do things like get one of our lads to bring in some beers for me, or a bottle of whisky. I was bored stupid in there and, the way I saw it, I was in there to get off heroin so it didn't matter if I had a drink. But they had to explain to me that there were real serious alcoholics in there, and they could smell the alcohol even if it was stashed in my room. I wasn't in the right frame of mind to be told what to do back then. I didn't listen to anyone, so I just went, 'Fuck it, then. I'm out of here,' and discharged myself and went home. Then, obviously, the first thing I did was get straight back on the gear. I just wasn't ready. I was still a kid really.

My second stint in rehab was after I came back from Barbados, recording *Yes Please!* Things had got a bit out of hand out there in Barbados. I was on methadone, which is a heroin substitute, before we went but I dropped my supply at Manchester airport, so in Barbados I ended up on crack cocaine. When I got back, the first thing I did was go straight into the Charter Clinic in London. We went to see a consultant and he told me I needed to be admitted for treatment. For once, I didn't need to be a specialist to make that diagnosis; it was obvious if I looked in a mirror. I was mentally and physically exhausted. I weighed about six stone wet through because I'd hardly eaten hardly anything for two months. I'd just been drinking and smoking crack and didn't want to eat. At the Charter Clinic they followed the twelve-step plan for addicts. It was pretty heavy on the religion, and even though I come from a Catholic background I thought it was a bit off-putting for people who are trying to come off drugs to have to go through the whole God thing. But I did take it a bit more seriously this time. They had this big American dude who started lecturing us about what he called 'Stinking Thinking'. His theory was when you're coming down you start thinking bad thoughts and he called it 'Stinking Thinking'. My ears picked up and I thought, 'I'm having that.' I knew straight away it could work as a lyric, and suddenly I'm writing lyrics in there, and 'Stinkin' Thinkin'' ended up being our next single.

The next time I tried, a few years later, I'd heard about these new naltrexone implants, which were supposed to be a wonder drug, so I decided to give them a try and booked myself into this clinic in London. Naltrexone was horrific. A living nightmare. It sounded great beforehand – they said they'd put you to sleep for twenty-four hours and speed up your withdrawal so you go through the worst while you're out of it. But it didn't work for me. I woke up, ripped all the tubes out and started going mental. It took half a dozen doctors and nurses to hold me down on the bed. I went fucking berserk. So that didn't work either.

In the end, it wasn't any fancy rehab that got me clean. I did on my own, with the help of my wife Joanne when we got back together. I cleaned myself up. I stopped taking cocaine, methadone and weed, and even stopped drinking for a while. I was completely straight, and started doing a lot of thinking. Thinking about all the things I'd buried since I was a kid. All the things I'd seen and done in Happy Mondays and Black Grape. Twenty years of life that I hadn't really had feelings about because I was anaesthetized by heroin. I then had to try and process all this shit. It was like fast-forwarding through twenty years of feelings. I was all over the place. Up and down like a fucking yo-yo. I felt like a ball in a mental pinball machine.

You have to process what happens to you eventually, mentally. Everyone does. Whether you're a rock star or a bin man. Otherwise it all catches up with you at some stage. I'm not naive. Even though I hadn't been ready for rehab when I was in there, I'd picked up on some bits of the counselling, which I'm sure helped me when I came to deal with it myself. I knew I had to deal with all those twenty years of emotions. No way round it. If you block something out it will catch up with you and eventually start dragging you down.

Through all that rehab and cold turkey, I've had to do so much self-analyzing and reflecting that I'm now pretty sure of who I am and how I got here today. I'm much more comfortable in my own skin now than I was twenty years ago, and a better person to be around because of it, and hopefully a better husband and dad. I'm not running away from anything and I'm happier than I've ever been. You have to find a way that works for you. Find out a way of resolving your issues that works for you. All I'd say is it's worth it in the end.

# Fame

F ame is a funny old game. I never set out to be famous or dreamed of being famous when I was a kid, that was never the aim. What I wanted to be was in a successful band, and I just realized that fame was something that came along with being in a successful band. It was really a by-product.

When I was kid, people were famous for being good at something. You were famous because you were a rock'n'roll star or because you played for Man United or because you were a great film star. Nowadays, you get these kids who are just famous for being famous, and that's all they want. That's their main focus. They don't want to be in a band or be a footballer or a DJ or whatever and get famous for doing that. They just want to be famous, pure and simple. I struggle to get my head round it. Reality TV stars who are just famous for being on *Love Island* or something. Or Instagram bloody 'influencers', whatever that means.

Half the time being famous is a pain in the arse. It just means people hassling you. In fact, I'd say being famous is a pain in the arse more often than not and only maybe 10 per cent or 20 per cent of the time do you actually see the benefit.

Some people want people looking at them all the time. They want to walk in a restaurant or hotel and have people turning and looking at them, whispering to their mates, 'Look who it is, over there.' I never wanted that side of it. I wasn't even that comfortable with people staring at me when I was on stage performing, let alone when I was just in a bar having a cheeky pint or at Asda doing the weekly shop or whatever.

It was when we first did *Top of the Pops* that I realized I was actually famous. That was a real turning point back then. You've got to remember this was before social media, before the internet, before camera phones, when pretty much everyone still only had four TV channels at home. You forget that people only really started getting satellite TV when the Premier League started, so back in 1990 most people still only had four TV channels, and being on *Top of the Pops* was a huge thing. When we went down to do *Top of the Pops* for the first time, people wanted to open the door for me. That's when I realized that things had changed and life probably wasn't going to be the same for me ever again. It's TV that changes things. You can be in a pretty successful band and, as long as you're not the singer, you can still live a normal life. A band like the Foo Fighters, say. They're a huge band who have been going for years now and sell out stadiums all over the world, but I bet the bass player can walk down the street without getting hassled, because hardly anyone knows what he looks like apart from the real hardcore fans. Dave Grohl, the singer, can't walk down the street but I bet the bass player and the drummer can. But you go and do a bit of reality TV and more people recognize you than Morrissey.

Funnily enough, after we became famous, we were always treated better in London than in Manchester. Probably down to two things – firstly, they don't like it in Manchester if you get too big for your boots. Which we never did but, even if you stay exactly the same, there'll always be some people who think that you've changed. Guy Garvey, the lead singer of Elbow, said that the day after they won the Mercury Music Prize, he got back to Manchester and was crossing the road in the middle of town, and a taxi driver beeped his horn and leaned out of the window and shouted, 'Elbow! Get a proper fucking job!'

The other reason we got treated better in London is we had a bit of a reputation round town in Manchester, and a lot of the bar owners and club owners just saw the scally reputation of the band and saw us as part of the drug scene. They didn't treat us like musicians. They treated us like people who were coming in off the street to sell drugs on their premises. Seriously. It didn't matter that we'd been on *Top of the Pops* and had records in the charts and were selling out the biggest venues in town; they just treated us like drug dealers and scallies who had caused them trouble. Down in London we were treated as musicians – and successful musicians. We were treated as though we were famous. People would open doors for you and welcome you in, but it was sometimes the opposite in Manchester. People would go out of their way to do anything for us in London, but people would often go out of their way to avoid us in Manchester. I'm not talking about the punters and the kids – they were always cool with us – but the bar owners and club owners. That's one of the reasons we'd spend so much time in Dry Bar, because it was owned by Factory and we didn't get treated like scallies in there. I mean Dry Bar was basically our front room for a while. We lived in there. We'd be in there every day. We even shot videos in the upstairs there.

A couple of times when I was back in Salford after the Mondays first became famous, I'd bump into an old mate from school and they were slightly off with me, as if they were waiting for me to start behaving like the Charlie-Big-Potatoes pop star, even though I never did that. But now I've moved back there, it's totally cool if I bump into someone I knew from school. The only weird thing is I might not recognize them if I haven't seen them since they were a teenager, because obviously they've changed a lot in those forty years. So have I but, because they've seen me on TV or in the press over the years, they don't think I've changed a bit.

To be honest, the main bonus of fame for me back in the day was that it stopped people presuming I was a drug dealer or I was going to rob the gaff. That used to happen all the time. Still does sometimes. I've got one of those faces. If I walked into a bank or went to buy a car or even a fucking train ticket, if the person behind the counter didn't recognize me, then they always treated me like shit because they took one look at me and presumed I was a drug dealer. It didn't help that I was usually paying cash. I don't so much these days, but certainly back in the day I would always pay cash. I just preferred using cash back then, but people think the only people carrying big wedges of cash are drug dealers or bank robbers. When it happens now, I just look around to see if any of the other staff have recognized me, and hopefully the manager or someone will clock me and come over and go 'Ah, Shaun Ryder!' and then the prick who has been treating me like shit is totally embarrassed.

When it comes to fame, there's really only two bands where everyone can name all the band members, and that's The Beatles and the Stones. Everyone knows John, Paul, George and Ringo. Mick, Keith, Charlie and Ronnie, as they are now. They're the only two bands that *everyone* knows, of any era. Maybe The Who at a stretch, although your mam wouldn't know what the bass player in The Who was called. Maybe the bloody Spice Girls, but only because they've all got short catchy nicknames. Most people couldn't even name all the fucking Bee Gees, and they're all brothers! I bet most people would struggle to remember all their first names. Same with The Jackson 5. Nobody can name The Kinks apart from Ray and Dave Davies. Everyone knows who Noddy Holder and Slade are, but tell me what the drummer was called? Everyone knows Morrissey and Johnny Marr, but only big Smiths fans know who the other two are. Same with New Order – everyone knew Bernard, and probably Hooky, but not many people knew who the other two were. They even made a joke of it by starting their own band called The Other Two when Bernard fucked off to do Electronic and Hooky started Revenge. Factory held a huge gig at G-Mex as part of the Festival of the Tenth Summer in 1986, which New Order headlined, and Stephen Morris couldn't even get into the gig. His own gig! When he turned up at the door they said he wasn't on the guest list. Stephen is the drummer in New Order (and before that, Joy Division) – great drummer and a lovely bloke – but he couldn't get into half his own gigs. At the Festival of Tenth Summer, Morrissey just waltzed past and in, as if he owned the gaff, so Stephen said to the guy, 'I might be down as Stephen Morrissey,' and Morrissey's name was on the list so Stephen Morris got in that way. He's the only member of New Order to have his face on one of their album covers, on *Low-Life*, but apparently even when they were touring that album he struggled to get in to some gigs, even though his face was on the album artwork on the tour passes.

Name one member of Madness apart from Suggs. Who are the rest of Guns N' Roses apart from Axl Rose and Slash? How many people know who's in U2 apart from Bono and the Edge? It's the same now – most people can't name all the members of Coldplay or Arctic Monkeys. That's just the way it is. If you want people to know who you are, and you want the attention and the adulation, don't play the bass or drums. It's that simple. You need to be the front man or maybe the lead guitarist. Or, in Bez's case, the fucking maracas. Although most maracas players don't get the attention Bez gets, obviously. That said, most maracas players would be hiding at the back, not down the front of the stage, dancing like a loon, with their eyes on stalks. The irony is, I didn't want the attention or the adulation. I enjoyed all the trappings that came with it, but if I hadn't had brought Bez in then I would have had to shoulder all the attention on my own, because it wouldn't have been me and the keyboard player.

The thing is, most people in bands have egos of some sort. You have to have some sort of ego to get up on stage and think people should be listening to your music in the first place. It's quite rare to find someone in a band that is happy to be in the shadows, so there's always a bit of resentment that someone else is getting more attention than you, from my experience. It goes back to *Stardust* again. When the band in *Stardust* become famous, David Essex's character is getting all the attention because he's the front man. He's the only one the press want to speak to, and they're treating the band as his backing band. The rest of the band get pissed off about him getting all the attention and you see them throwing darts at pictures of David Essex. I'd seen this film when I was thirteen, and then formed a band and got to live it, and all these clichés came true. Even as the band took off, when you should be enjoying the ride, all these things started to happen and all of a sudden I'm like, 'Well, *this* is a fucking cliché… and *that* turned out to be true…' It was like rock'n'roll-cliché bingo, and you feel like you're powerless to stop it happening. I don't think the rest of the band ever threw darts at pictures of me or Bez, but they might as well have done.

We had every rock'n'roll cliché going on at the end of the Mondays. We had all the sex and drugs and rock'n'roll. We had the egos all battling against each other, and everyone getting a bit too big for their boots. We had the rest of the band hating the lead singer for getting all the attention. We had the Yoko thing going on, with people wanting to bring wives and girlfriends into the studio when the band were supposed to be working. We had people in the band throwing their toys out of the pram and wanting to split the band up after we got our first bad review in the press… Seriously, we had every fucking cliché going. We were throwing away everything that we had worked so hard for. We were playing rock'n'roll-bingo, and we had a full house! I was like, 'Fucking hell, you've all seen *Stardust*. You've all read the books about The Beatles splitting up. Can't you see what's happening?'

I get recognized and approached everywhere. It's just how you deal with it that matters. When I'm back home, I keep myself to myself with my family, pretty much. I don't really go out locally. If me and Joanne go out, we'll go to a restaurant for something to eat and that's it. We don't go to clubs or pubs, which is where you would get more hassle. But if I'm working in Manchester or down in London, doing TV or press, then I might go in somewhere for a quick drink, and then I'll always get someone coming over. The thing is, people still presume I want to party.

People's heads just go somewhere else when they see someone famous. Their heads go to mush. Not just your average bloke on the street – it happens with coppers and everyone. I'll give you one example: I was on Salford Precinct a few years ago, when my youngest girls were toddlers. Jo had just popped in the shop or something and left me with both of them, so I'm there doing my best to control two toddlers by a busy road, with cars flying past, and there's workmen on the pavement with pneumatic drills digging a 20-foot hole, and this female copper spots me and starts hassling me for a selfie and to sign something for her sister. The kids have wriggled free and I'm chasing them and trying to grab them and stop them falling down this big hole, and all this copper's arsed about is chasing me for a selfie, rather than helping me make sure the kids are OK.

My two youngest girls have grown up with fame. They're used to seeing me on the TV, it's just Dad's job. They come to some of our gigs, and *it's just Dad's job.* When they were little they just sort of accepted it but, now they're older and becoming teenagers, they're not afraid of saying something. If we're out for a bite to eat and someone comes over, hassling me for a selfie during the meal, I would probably do it but the girls will say something pointed like, 'We're out with *our dad...*' or 'We're trying to eat.'

It's hard to give advice on how to handle fame when it happens, because it's such a fucking weird thing. It's so weird to suddenly have everyone treating you differently, especially if you have a bit of self-doubt like I did back then. There probably are some rock stars who get famous and think, '*Finally*, everyone is treating me the way I deserve to be treated!' but I wasn't one of them. I don't think anything can prepare you for fame, and everyone handles it differently. The weird thing is it becomes normal after a while. You just get used to it and find a way of handling it. You also find a way of swerving it if you want to. I know where I'll be recognized and hassled the most, so I just avoid those places a lot of the time, if I'm not in the mood.

It also gets easier to handle as you get older. When you're younger you can question yourself and think, 'Do I deserve this? Is this who I am now?' When you're older, it doesn't bother you so much. You don't question yourself like that, because you're more at peace with yourself and you know who you are and that the fame thing is just all smoke and mirrors really. It doesn't affect who you are when you get home and shut the front door.

# Rivalries

I 've never felt a direct rivalry with any band, really. With both Happy Mondays and Black Grape, I was always determined for us to be unique and different from anyone else, rather than directly competing with anyone. I'm not saying I wasn't competitive. You have to be pretty driven to get anywhere in this game, and obviously when you first start out, you're competing with other bands for gigs, and then later on for festival slots or TV appearances or whatever, but I never saw any band as a direct rival. Not like The Beatles and the Stones, or Oasis and Blur, although that was a bit manufactured.

When the Mondays first broke through, we were obviously part of the whole Madchester scene, and some people presumed there must have been some rivalry with the other bands, particularly The Stone Roses maybe, but there was absolutely no rivalry with them from my side. There really wasn't. At the time, the Roses did use to go around saying stuff in interviews like, 'We're the best band in the world!' and all that, but I'd just think, 'Right, OK. If they like saying that, fine.' That was just their vibe in interviews, and it was more aimed at huge bands like U2 than us. Besides, the Roses would never say anything like that in person. They were all really good lads, really sound. I first got to know Ian Brown when we lived near each other in Fallowfield in the late eighties, and me and him would often meet up at the local McDonalds in the afternoon, which was usually when I was just getting up. So the Mondays were good mates with the Roses, but we didn't hang around with them all the time. The Roses didn't seem to party that much. Apart from Mani. But he did enough partying for all four of them! I always thought their best move was bringing Mani in. They were a good band before he joined, but Mani seemed to be the final link. That was when they stepped up a gear and became a great band. I didn't see them live much because we were off doing our own thing, but I did go to their huge Spike Island gig, although I can't really remember it. I think everyone's memories of that day are a bit hazy.

The Roses were the same with us – they didn't see us as rivals that they needed to be wary of. Ian said he used to buzz off the Mondays, and he actually once came out and said 'Happy Mondays are the best band in Manchester.' Some journalists might have thought there was a bit of rivalry there, but there really wasn't. Things were pretty tight between us. If we were going off on tour and had a bit of a party the night before in Manchester, the Roses would be there at the party to see us off.

Looking back, I was pretty horrible about Inspiral Carpets a couple of times, back in the day, but that was just because I didn't want to be roped in with them. I didn't want to be roped in with anyone really. I knew it would only hold us back in the end if we were pigeonholed with other bands. I do remember once sending nasty faxes over to their keyboard player, Clint Boon, at the Inspirals office, saying 'You bunch of tossers...' and stuff like that. Then we started getting quite naughty faxes back, saying 'You bunch of dicks...' I couldn't fucking believe it when those faxes came through! It was fine for us to give them shit, but I didn't expect Clint to give it back! I thought, 'You cheeky bastard, I'll put you in a box!' Then I found out, years later, that it was actually their roadie at the time who was sending all these faxes – Noel bloody Gallagher!

Noel started off as the Inspirals' roadie, before he was in Oasis, and toured the world with them. It must have been quite weird for the Inspirals to then watch their roadie go on and be a bigger rock star than they had ever been but, to be fair to them, they've always been pretty cool about it. Clint Boon is now a good friend of mine, and he's a really lovely bloke, so I feel bad about saying horrible stuff back in the day, but I was just a kid really. I might have been in my late twenties but I was so young, and I just didn't want to be roped in with anyone.

Noel and Oasis then went on to have a massive rivalry with Blur in the nineties, and that didn't do either of them any harm, although it was more their record labels fuelling that rivalry than the bands themselves. Their battle for No. 1 was cooked up by the record companies really, and it worked, as it was the lead item on the *Nine O'Clock News*. Noel and Damon are friendly now and have even done stuff together.

Even The Beatles had a bit of a rivalry with the Stones, and The Beach Boys. Lennon and McCartney wrote one of the Stones' first hits for them, 'I Wanna Be Your Man', but as the Stones became bigger they became rivals. The Beach Boys and The Beatles, on the other hand, had the type of creative rivalry where each album one band released just spurred the other band on to up their game. They both started off as quite clean-cut bands, and both started to get more far out. When Brian Wilson heard *Rubber Soul*, he was blown away and it inspired him to go away and write *Pet Sounds*. Then when McCartney heard *Pet Sounds*, he was blown away and decided he wanted the next Beatles album to be even more ambitious, and came up with the idea of *Sgt Pepper's*. You're talking about two of the greatest albums ever made, so some good can come out of rivalries.

As for me, I certainly don't have any rivalry with anyone nowadays. I'm much more relaxed than I was back in the day, and once you've been in the rock'n'roll game as long as I have, I think there's mostly a mutual respect for any other band who has lasted as long as you have. Even if you're not really into the music, you think, 'Fair play, mate. You're still here thirty years later, when so many other bands have dropped by the wayside and been forgotten about.'

# Interviews

Some musicians love giving interviews, as they love nothing more than the sound of their own voice and they think the world needs to know their opinion on anything and everything. There's a few other musicians, even really famous ones, who might look confident on stage but clam up as soon as a journalist sticks a Dictaphone or microphone in front of then, and just give one-word answers. I'm somewhere in between.

I've never been one of those who was looking for a platform to spout my opinions, but I knew early on the value of doing press and very quickly realized we could get a lot more press if we didn't mind playing the game. The Mondays quickly got a rock'n'roll reputation and it was very obvious to me that it would work in our favour if we played up to that. It wasn't even playing up to it, because that's what we were really like. It was more a case of simply not hiding it from the press. If we were doing an interview in a pub with

157

*NME* or whoever back then, if Bez or me chopped out a line on the pool table or rolled a spliff during the interview, the interview would then turn into a big feature over several pages. It was that simple. The press couldn't get enough of it because there was no one else like us around at the time. We'd grown up on all these rock'n'roll tales of the sixties and the seventies but, by the time we came along in the eighties, everything had become really clean-cut. It was like punk had never happened, so people were desperate for someone who was a bit more rock'n'roll.

So that really worked for us, and the band are remembered for the music and our rock'n'roll behaviour. Now if I'm interviewed by someone like the *Guardian* they'll want to ask about the lyrics or the inspiration behind the music, whereas if I'm interviewed by a tabloid newspaper you can guarantee they'll be looking for some good old tales of rock'n'roll, even though I don't party like I used to. The sex, drugs and rock'n'roll image of the Mondays always came hand in hand with the music for me. Over thirty years later, people still love the Mondays' music but they also want to talk about our rock'n'roll tales. Maybe without those rock'n'roll tales and us being so infamous, the music wouldn't have got the attention it deserved and might have been forgotten about. I've long given up that rock'n'roll lifestyle, but I don't mind being asked about it. It's part of the Mondays and Black Grape image and package, I get that. People still love a good rock'n'roll story about me or Bez, and they don't mind if it's one that's twenty or thirty years old. As long as the music gets appreciated as well, I'm fine with that.

Once you're on a record label and start releasing records, you usually have a PR or press officer who will handle all your press. They're responsible for press releases and handling interview requests from journalists and all that side of things. We were quite lucky in that our first two press officers for Happy Mondays were Dave Harper and then Jeff Barrett, who were both nutcases who totally got the Mondays. They didn't try and concoct some cock-and-bull story around the band – they totally got that the band *were* the story, that there was no need to dress it up because our real lives were far more rock'n'roll and shocking than anything they could cook up. It was great and refreshing to work with them. After having dealt with some dickheads in the industry telling us we needed to get an image, here were two guys who knew that the Mondays already had the best image possible, and they could work with that. Jeff believed in us more than anyone in the early days, and even before he started doing our press, he organized a lot of our early gigs in London. Jeff was also as full-on as us when it came to partying. He went on to form Heavenly Recordings and put out a lot of great records by bands like Saint Etienne, Flowered Up, the Manics and loads of others. Heavenly are still going thirty years later, signing young bands like Working Men's Club.

I'm getting sidetracked, but my point was it's great to work with a press officer who gets the band, and helps get the press on your side, or at least sees the band for what they really are. The other thing I realized for myself early on is that if you've been open from the start about your lifestyle and things like drug use, then it can't catch up on you. Tony Wilson used to actively encourage that sort of behaviour from us. It was one of the bonuses about being on Factory Records for us. He absolutely loved it, although I'm not sure the rest of Factory did as much. People like Hooky from New Order certainly didn't. He thought you should keep that sort of stuff under wraps (no pun intended), even though he used to party pretty bloody hard as well. New Order were hardly squeaky clean. They were no saints, although they never got involved in hard drugs like I did. It might have been different if we had been on a major record label, where they might have had a more draconian attitude and taken us aside and said, 'Listen, you can't keep banging on about selling drugs and taking drugs,' but Tony Wilson encouraged it. After we had been so open about it, then it became easier for other bands to come after us and talk openly about taking drugs. When Oasis started, I remember Noel saying that taking drugs was as normal as having a cup of tea. I'm not sure he would have got away with saying that if we hadn't already talked about it so openly a few years before.

We got our first ever front cover in 1986, for *Melody Maker* for our debut album. I knew we were going to be on the front cover, so the morning that *Melody Maker* came out (OK, maybe the afternoon it came out!) I was down the local paper shop to buy it. I knew the guy in the shop thought I was a dodgy scally, as he always kept his eye on me when I went in there, as if I was going to rob the place, so I was looking forward to seeing his face when I put *Melody Maker* on the counter with me on the cover. But when I got down there and picked it up, they'd used this picture of me and Bez with our hoods up, so you couldn't really see it was me anyway. Could have been anyone!

You can't really interview five members of a band at once because either it gets a bit unruly, with people shouting over each other, or one or two people dominate the interview and the others just sit there. After our first few interviews, it ended up usually just being me and Bez doing the interviews, which the rest of the band were fine with because they couldn't be arsed and didn't have much to say anyway. It wasn't until later, when me and Bez became much more famous than them, that they got resentful about it. The egos come in to play, and it was egos that eventually split the Mondays up. Everyone thinks it was the drugs and madness that split the Mondays but, trust me, it was egos. The seed was sown when the band started to get a lot more attention, and me and Bez ended up doing most of the interviews and, next thing you know, it's me and Bez on the front of the *NME* and other magazines. Then when we turn up to do *Top of the Pops*, people open the door for me and Bez, because they recognize us and know who we are, and then it shuts behind us, in the face of the rest of the band, because no one recognizes them. So their noses get put out of joint and all of a sudden they wanted to do interviews, which I was fine with. Fine, you do the interviews, then. But the journalists didn't want to speak to them, because Mark Day would just talk about his guitar playing and what key he was in or whatever, Paul Davis would just babble utter nonsense, and our kid would be trying to come across really intelligent but was just a bit boring. You'd send them to speak to the *NME* and you'd only get a half-page or a page feature out of it, whereas if me and Bez went and did the interview we'd end up on the front cover and a five-page feature because we gave them exactly what they wanted.

The only thing that really bothered me about interviews after they were printed was when they used to quote me or Bez and instead of writing 'fuck' they'd put 'fook'. That used to wind me right up. It was one thing that really did my fucking head in. Not my 'fookin' head in. It didn't even look or sound right, 'fook' or 'fookin' just looked fucking ridiculous.

I was never bothered about who was coming to interview us. Some of the bigger music journalists had reputations, but I honestly couldn't have cared less. For instance, I remember it was supposed to be a big deal when Nick Kent came down to *Top of the Pops* to do a big piece on us and the Roses for *The Face*. It might have been to some student band, but I couldn't have cared less. To me, he was just some journalist that Sid Vicious once beat up. There was a bit of an issue when the magazine came out because he quoted Wilson saying, 'I have absolutely no problem with any of these guys dying on me. Ian Curtis committing suicide is the best thing that ever happened to me. Death sells.' Wilson got upset and said he didn't say it, and I believed him, but it didn't bother me. It's the sort of thing Wilson might have said, and the sort of thing I would have come out with back then too, so I wasn't really arsed.

There were a few music journalists who were decent sorts. Jack Barron from the *NME* was as mental as we were. I was almost shocked when I found out a few years ago that he was still alive, as he seemed on a self-destruct mission more than us. I believe he's not been well over the last couple of years, so I hope he's OK. James Brown was also at the *NME* then, and he was a big champion of ours early on. He did some great live reviews of our early gigs, and then a bit later we took him on tour with us to Brazil. Both Jack and James were caners at the time, they used to party as hard as us, so maybe that's why we got on with them. They've both been sober for a while now. Back then, if any journalists were coming with us on tour or on a foreign trip, all we were bothered about was if they would be a good laugh and up for anything. We didn't want any journalists around that were going to cramp our style. If you're coming on tour with the Mondays, then you need to get on the bus, if you know what I mean.

After you've been on *Top of the Pops* and in the charts, then the tabloids all of a sudden become interested in you. Particularly if they can smell anything they can sell as a bit of controversy or gossip. Back then, the tabloids didn't really cover music at all. A few years later, in the mid-nineties, when bands like us and then Oasis, Blur and Pulp had taken over the charts, there became more of a celebrity culture around music, and all the tabloids started up music and celeb pages, like the Bizarre column or the 3AM Girls. A lot of journalists like Piers Morgan or Gordon Smart first made their name as a celebrity reporter. But when we first broke through, it was more unusual for a band like us to give an interview to a tabloid. It was a bit frowned upon in the music industry. Some people thought it wasn't cool, that you should just stick to speaking to the *NME*, and would warn us off the tabloids, saying stuff like 'They'll just twist what you say. They'll big you up and then do a number on you.' But I never agreed with all that bollocks. That was small-time thinking, student thinking to me. We wanted to get into the tabloids and reach as many people as possible. Any two-bit student indie band can get in the *NME*. We didn't want to just reach students, we wanted to attract as many people as possible.

When the press did turn on us a bit for the first time, towards the end of the Mondays, the rest of the band couldn't handle it and blamed me and Bez for it. I knew it was going to come at some stage, and was more like, 'Hang on a minute, we've had a good fucking run with the press. They were going to have a dig at us at some stage.' We'd almost never have a bad review in the press until *Yes Please!* came out and then, the first time it happens, the rest of them want to split the fucking band up and throw everything away that we'd worked for. None of our songs or albums had ever been torn to bits, we'd always got good reviews. But it's just part of the game, you know? It's your turn to get a kicking. And that's what happened to us, it was just due. You look at any band who's had longevity and they've all had a kicking in their time. Even the biggest bands in the world – like the Rolling Stones or U2 – have had their periods when they definitely weren't cool and everyone was giving them a bit of a kicking in the press, and then things come back round again and they're back in favour. It's the same with any artists in the public eye. Actors or film directors or authors or whoever – no one gets a free ride all the way, everyone gets a kicking at one stage or another. Same in sport, United fans even wanted Alex Ferguson out at one stage, and the press were writing him off, despite everything he'd won, and then he turned it round again and won another few trophies and all of a sudden the fans were singing Fergie's name again and the same journalists who were saying he was finished were saying he was the greatest manager ever. It happens to *everyone*, so when it happens to you, you've just got to roll with it. If you throw the towel in when you get your first bit of bad press, then you ain't gonna last long in this game, mate.

Believe it or not, I actually had a short journalism career myself, when I had a column in the *Daily Sport* in the late nineties, although I didn't write it myself. A guy called John Warburton, or Warbie, used to ghostwrite it for me, and I got quite pally with him. The column all came about from when I was going cold turkey to get off heroin at my old mate Too Nice Tom's house in Burnley. One of Tom's mates was Tony Livesey, who was then editor of the *Daily Sport* and now presents the drive-time show on Radio 5 Live. Tom and Tony were old mates from college and Tony came round to Tom's one day when I was staying there, and we all got chatting and he ended up offering me a column in the paper.

That all led on to the time when I pulled a gun on a journalist. Or so the story goes. It was some young guy from the *Manchester Evening News*. It sounds much worse on paper than it actually was. Yet again, it was just one of those stories that got blown out of proportion. The incident ended up being on the front page of the *Evening News*, with them claiming I pulled a gun on their reporter. Which was just stupid sensationalism. It was just a joke that got out of hand, but the *Evening News* obviously couldn't believe their luck, and were rubbing their hands about running with the headline 'Shaun Ryder pulled a gun on me!'

It all started when Warbie asked if I would do a book with him. I wasn't ready to do a book at that time, but I got on all right with Warbie and told him that if he wanted to do a book about me, I was fine with that. So he went off and wrote it, and when it was coming out he asked me to come down to the launch at Waterstones on Deansgate in Manchester. There was a journalist from the *Evening News* there who wanted to interview me, and I wasn't really in the mood, so I just started having a bit of a nobble with him, winding him up, and then I pulled out this plastic gun and he fucking shit himself. It was just a little plastic starter pistol. I don't even remember where I got it from. I think I'd found it just before we got to Waterstones. I certainly wasn't carrying a gun around with me. It was just a toy. It might as well have had one of those flags that came out at the end and said 'Bang!' Any idiot who'd seen a real gun would know this was a toy, but this journalist shit it and I ended up on the front page of the bloody *Evening News*: 'Shaun Ryder pulled a gun on me!'

It was just another Shaun Ryder myth to add to the list.

# Video shoots

Video shoots are one of those things you have to do as a musician that most of the time aren't half as glamorous as they look. If you think photoshoots can drag on, video shoots are just a double-long photoshoot. Depending on the budget and the director, some of the bigger music videos can take several days or a week to shoot, and there's a lot of hanging around. Thankfully, a lot of our video shoots didn't take as long as that, and we were lucky to mostly work with directors that we got on with.

A lot of musicians feel a bit of a dick when they first make music videos, prancing around in front of the camera with no audience there. Just when you're starting to get over being self-conscious about doing it on stage with an audience, you then have to go and do it in front of the cameras and no audience, which makes you feel ridiculous all over again. Unless you're a complete narcissist like Kanye West, you're obviously going to feel a bit of a tit at first, until you just accept that it's all a bit ridiculous and just go with it. I bet The Beatles felt absolutely ridiculous when they were making *Help!*, going down a dry ski slope, doing semaphore with the flags and all that, but you do have to go with it.

Even David Bowie felt like a bit of a tit at times. There's a great story about when he was filming the video for 'Ashes to Ashes' in 1980, which cost £250,000 and was the most expensive music video ever made at that time. It was filmed on a beach in Sussex, with Bowie wearing a clown suit and being followed by a bulldozer. The way Bowie told it (as reported by Michael Dignum, crew member on the shoot, to BowieBible):

> It's easy to get caught up in the hype. It changes you. So I was on the set of the music video 'Ashes To Ashes', do you know the one? So we're on the beach shooting this scene with a giant bulldozer. The camera was on a very long lens. In this video I'm dressed from head to toe in a clown suit. Why not? I hear playback and the music starts.
>
> So off I go, I start singing and walking, but as soon as I do this old geezer with an old dog walks right between me and the camera.
>
> Well, knowing this is gonna take a while I walked past the old guy and sat next to camera in my full costume waiting for him to pass. As he is walking by the camera the director said, 'Excuse me mister, do you know who

this is?' The old guy looks at me from bottom to top and looks back to the director and said:

'Of course I do! It's some cunt in a clown suit.'

That was a huge moment for me. It put me back in my place and made me realize, yes, I'm just a cunt in a clown suit. I think about that old guy all the time.

So, you know, once you know that even Bowie sometimes felt like a cunt in a clown suit when he was making a video, then you don't feel so bad!

The first video we ever made with Happy Mondays was for 'Tart Tart', the first single from our debut album, *Squirrel and G-Man*. It was directed by a Mancunian duo of filmmakers, Keith Jobling and Phil Shotton, who called themselves the Bailey Brothers. I got on with them straight away, as we were on a similar vibe and were big fans of all the same films – *Performance* and stuff like that. Not long after I met him, I remember saying to Keith, 'Have you seen *Thief*?' which was a seventies American film about a professional thief, starring James Caan, that I was really into. Keith was like, 'No way, man! I'm always mentioning that film to people and no one else has ever seen it!' Keith knew his films and I knew my films, and we could talk about them for ages, so I felt they were right for the Mondays, and felt comfortable working with them. I really got on with them, and they went on to direct almost all of Happy Mondays' videos. I still see them now and again. Keith now designs websites and he did a Mondays website for us a few years ago when we first reformed, and Phil is still involved in film too.

We shot that first video at Strawberry Studios in Stockport, the recording studios built by 10cc with the money they made from 'I'm Not In Love'. Fair play to them for investing back into a place like Stockport where bands from all over the North West could use it. Most Manchester bands at the time had recorded there, including Joy Division, Buzzcocks, James, The Smiths, the Roses and even St Winifred's School Choir, who were from St Winifred's primary school in Stockport and recorded that song 'There's No One Quite Like Grandma', which was Christmas No.1 in 1980 and they even got on *Top of the Pops* with it.

I didn't want to mime in the video for 'Tart Tart' because I felt ridiculous. It's a very weird thing to do when you first get asked to do it. Back then, lots of artists like The Clash refused to mime as they thought it was cheating or selling out. So I came up with this great idea that I would mime out of time, as I thought it would be obvious I was taking the mick out of the whole charade. In my head I thought it would look cool and be seen as a statement. It didn't. It just looked shit. I looked like a bit of a goon who didn't know what he was doing, or that I was so munted that I couldn't even mime to my own song. So that was the last time I made that mistake. When we came to make the next video, I'd got my head around the whole miming thing.

The video to 'Tart Tart' did get on *The Chart Show*, which was a big deal to us. If you don't remember, *The Chart Show* was on Saturday mornings on ITV and was the only show on television at the time that showed the indie charts – and we were in the indie charts. That was our first experience of our video being shown on nationwide television. I remember being sat at home watching the indie chart run-down on Saturday morning, and there we were, Happy Mondays on Saturday-morning TV, which was great. That really did seem a big step for us at the time. That's where I wanted us to be, on mainstream TV.

The video to our next single, '24 Hour Party People', was another Bailey Brothers job, shot in Manchester. It's basically the Mondays bombing around town in an Oldsmobile, which was a big old American car that was owned by some guy that Tony Wilson knew who collected classic American cars. We're all just crammed in the car, and I'm crushed in the back seat, with the camera right in my face, miming. The little kid pretending to drive the car at the start is Mark Bradbury, who was the little brother of Suzy, who was my girlfriend at the time. Mark still lives just round the corner from me in Salford now, near to Ryan Giggs. Mark was only about ten or eleven when we shot that video; he's in his mid-forties now and he's got about nine kids. He's actually done all right for himself, he's a proper entrepreneur type.

We never looked at music videos by other bands for inspiration, we were more inspired by off-beat films like *Performance* and stuff like that. When we came to record *Bummed* acid house was taking off in Manchester, and when we came to shoot the video for 'Wrote For Luck' we really wanted to capture the feeling of those early acid house days and the parties and raves that were happening, because that's what we were bang into at the time, that's where our heads were at. We shot it with Bailey Brothers at Legends, a great club in Manchester that's not there any more. Greg Wilson used to DJ there and then Oakenfold later did his Spectrum club nights there. We just hired it out, and all the extras in the video are just our crew and the party people that we were knocking about with at the time.

*Everyone* was on ecstasy that night. It's so obvious if you look closely at it. If anyone turned up that night and wasn't on E, they soon got given one by one of our lot. It's quite a simple video but it really captures the trippy, underground, moody rave vibe in Manchester at that time. Which is a really hard thing to capture on film. Most of the rave scenes in films are shocking, really cringy efforts, and nothing like the real thing. But the Bailey Brothers did a great job of capturing that vibe. Full-on hedonism with a touch of menace underneath. When Factory knew what we were planning they were worried it might not get shown on TV because it was pretty overtly druggy, so they rounded up a bunch of local school kids and filmed an alternative, family-friendly version during the day, just featuring kids, then we all showed up in the evening to shoot the proper offside version.

You've got to remember that back then that scene was totally new and it was seen as really edgy, particularly by the media. They certainly didn't see it as a love-in. They were frightened of it because they didn't understand it. They would cross the road to avoid people like the Mondays and our crew. To be honest, quite a few of our crew and people involved did have an edge to them.

Fair play to the Bailey Brothers, they did a great job with all our videos, considering the tiny budgets they were working on, and they still stand up today. I think the budget was about £6000 for one of our videos, which was a tenth of the budget for a New Order video. Wilson also loved the Bailey Brothers, and together they came up with this idea for a Factory film called *Mad Fuckers*. It never saw the light of day, but we filmed a few scenes on the same day we shot the 'Wrote For Luck' video. Me and Bez were playing two mad fuckers, picking up a parcel from Donald Johnson from A Certain Ratio. I'm not sure anyone ever worked out what the film was about. Wilson did go over to Hollywood to try and get it financed, but it never got finished. Half of Manchester was supposedly going to be in *Mad Fuckers* at one stage and it now has a bit of a mythical status as 'the great lost Factory film' or something.

Another video we did with the Bailey Brothers that looked great was 'Lazyitis' as a single, with Karl Denver. We shot the video underneath the Mancunian Way. The idea was that we were all convicts, playing football in the rain in the prison yard. We got hold of some prison uniforms from Strangeways, but we ended up having to get a rain machine. Must have been the only time when it didn't fucking rain in Manchester. We shot it all on one night, and we had a few of our crew – John the Duck and people like that – in it playing football. It was freezing and we had the rain machine pissing down on us, so half of us ended up with colds and poor Karl Denver got pneumonia.

The Bailey Brothers weren't necessarily very commercial, but they really captured the Mondays music. The most commercial video we ever did was 'Step On'. A lot of people think it's filmed in Los Angeles for some reason, maybe because there's a shot in the video that is very similar to a shot where a plane takes off in the film *Bad Boys*, which is set in LA. Also because the sun is shining, and there's a palm tree in the opening shot, and when we're on the rooftop of the hotel, it looks more like the roof of a hotel in downtown LA, but it's actually shot in in Sitges, the gay capital of Spain, just outside Barcelona. We wanted to get the single out quick at the start of the summer, so not too much thought went into it. 'Step On' had a summery vibe to it, and we had a gig in Barcelona anyway, so we just filmed it in the sun on top of the hotel we were staying in at Sitges. They had huge letters spelling out 'H O T E L' so I climbed up on the E for a joke. Me on an E. The *NME* photographer Kevin Cummins was there, and he took a picture of me climbing the E and it was an *NME* front cover. They even gave it away as a poster too.

There was rarely any plot to the videos we shot with the Bailey Brothers, and they certainly weren't choreographed. They just shot us in the wild. A gang of cool guys on their hotel roof in the sun, with a bit of marijuana smoke drifting across the set. Job done. I got on with the Bailey Brothers, like I said, and we just trusted them. Keith Jobling said once about making Mondays videos: 'We used to get them to be completely natural and try and get as far away from them as we could, on a long lens, and film them like they were a pride of lions on the Serengeti – don't disturb them, just let them do their own thing.'

With the first Black Grape album, once we had decided that 'Reverend Black Grape' was the obvious choice for the first single, Kurfirst brought in Don Letts to do the video, who he was mates with because he had managed Big Audio

Dynamite in the past. Don Letts made total sense because he came from that background of mixing punk and reggae, which fitted perfectly with Black Grape. We filmed it on a housing estate in Ancoats in Manchester and then the interior scenes upstairs in Dry Bar. Ancoats at that time was nothing like it is now. Now it's full of flash loft apartments and craft-beer bars and artisanal delis. You'd struggle to buy a pint of milk round there back then. The video looked great, although I was really pissed off when I went home that day as some little fucker nicked a lovely Comme des Garçons blazer and a Gaultier jacket I had with me while we were filming in Dry Bar.

After the first Black Grape video worked out so good, we stuck with Don Letts again for the second Black Grape single, 'In the Name of the Father', although the budget had gone up a bit by then so we shot it in Jamaica rather than a housing estate in Manchester! I'd never been to Jamaica before, and it was a step up from bloody Ancoats. Don wanted to have us dressed as missionaries, with Carlos the Jackal, George Best and Pablo Escobar as our religious icons. I had to float down the river on this raft they'd built. We were there for about a week, and I just chilled out when we weren't filming. Kermit was off scoring crack and getting on it while we there, but for once I didn't partake. I just stuck to the Guinness and weed.

'Kelly's Heroes' was the third Black Grape single, and we ended up having to shoot two videos for that because the Americans didn't like the first one. They just didn't get it. The first one we shot in a club in London, with Bez dressed as Batman and me in a blonde wig. Patsy Kensit is in that one, and we filmed it just before she got together with Liam

Gallagher. The Americans didn't like it at all, so we then had to shoot a different one for them, which was like an armed bank-robbery scenario. By the time we came to film the second video, Kermit was ill with septicaemia. He actually got quite badly ill, after using dirty water when he was injecting heroin. So we brought in another rapper called Psycho as his replacement. Psycho's real name was Carl McCarthy, and he was a mate of Kermit's from Moss Side who had come down and done some additional vocals on 'In the Name of the Father' when we were recording the album. He was still at college and a DJ, and he had the right attitude and looked great. I didn't realize then that, after Kermit came back, him and Psycho would get it into their heads that they were Tupac and Biggie.

A couple of live videos of the Mondays came out, but we never did a behind-the-scenes type thing. But with Black Grape, a mate of mine, Too Nice Tom, wanted to make a documentary about us, right from me putting the band together and early rehearsals at my house in Didsbury, right through the recording of both albums, and going on tour and to America. It was called *The Grape Tapes* and it's a warts-and-all depiction of Black Grape. I've not seen it for a long time, but last time I saw some of it I just couldn't believe what I was seeing, or that we let Too Nice Tom get it all on film. It does capture the debauchery of Black Grape, but it doesn't exactly always depict me in the best light.

We shot a bit of a jokey video in Barcelona when I collaborated with Russell Watson on our cover version of 'Barcelona'. It's pretty obvious that the video and the song aren't totally serious, it's just playing up the juxtaposition of an opera singer against a bit of a wasted rock'n'roller. I'm just hamming it up a bit in the video, playing up to that caricature of the wasted Shaun Ryder against Russell's clean-cut image.

Of all the video shoots I've ever done, the Gorillaz one for 'DARE' was probably the biggest nightmare. It was just hard work. My weight can fluctuate a bit, and I was quite heavy at that stage. The idea for the video was that I didn't have a body, and I was just supposed to be this giant disembodied head, kept alive by a machine. Which meant I had to stay stuck in this box, with just my head peeking out the top, for hours on end. It was a long day. When I was recording the vocals, they couldn't get my levels right in my headphones, and I kept asking the engineer to turn it up. They ended up keeping the recording of me telling him, 'It's coming up, it's coming up,' and making that a major part of the track. It worked really well and they decided to make it the single, and it ended up going to No.1, which is my only No.1 single.

# Hotels

Some people might find it hard to believe, but I've never trashed a hotel room. I've trashed a few dressing rooms when I've been pissed off with a performance or something going wrong at a gig, but I've never trashed a hotel room. Quite a few hotel rooms have been trashed when the Mondays have been on tour in the past, but not by me, and not by the rest of the band either. If it happened it was one of our entourage, as there were some real naughty boys in our huge entourage at some stages, but I'm not being held responsible for their behaviour, and I'm certainly not paying for it when the hotel manager comes with the bill.

Keith Moon was one of the first to be obsessed with trashing hotel rooms. I did love that story about him leaving a hotel one morning, absolutely spannered, and then waking up in the back of the car in a panic and telling his driver to stop and turn around: 'I forgot something! We've got to go back!' When they got back to the hotel, Keith ran up to his room, grabbed the television and threw it out the window and into the swimming pool. Then he went back downstairs, got back in his car with a sigh of relief, and said to his driver, 'I nearly forgot.'

A lot of big rock stars use pseudonyms when they're on tour. Rod Stewart used to be Denis Law. We did use pseudonyms, but I can't for the life of me remember what they were. I struggled to remember what they were at the time, to be honest, although it was the tour manager who usually handled all that stuff anyway. You have a tour manager who basically tells you what's going on, and you don't even check into a hotel. The tour manager usually checks in for all of you, and then just hands out the keys and tells you what time you're leaving for the soundcheck or the gig, and what time the call is the next morning. And he'll probably get you all an alarm call or he'll call you himself – or, in my case, come and bash on your door to get you out of bed.

One of the reasons we used a tour manager, unlike other bands, is sometimes we used to get a loads of wrong-uns using our hotel rooms before us. Some of the lads who followed us around, our extended entourage, would get to the hotel before us and pretend they were us and check in to our rooms. We'd turn up knackered and needing to get our heads down for a bit of a kip before the gig, and these lads would already be in our fucking beds, sleeping off their hangovers! I bet that never happened to U2.

We stayed in some shitholes when we started out as a band. Every band does. But it never used to bother us, as we were young enough back then to still be on a buzz about being on the road, and we were wasted each night anyway.

I'd hardly ever stayed in a hotel before I was in a band. When I was a kid, when we went on holiday we used to go to Pontins, so it's not like we'd grown up staying in hotels. In the very early days, we'd go on tour in a rented Transit, and have to all kip in the back on top of each other, so any cheap hotel was a step up for us after that. The other thing was that, in the early days of the Mondays, most of us didn't really have a stable home to come back to anyway, so it's not like we were missing our home comforts. Bez and I shared a succession of flats that weren't great, and there were a few periods, even when the band took off, when I didn't have anywhere to kip at all. I was basically homeless and crashing on different people's sofas when we came back off tour. At least when we were on tour, you knew you were going to have a bed to kip in that night.

When we went down to London to record our debut album, with John Cale from The Velvet Underground in 1986, Factory put us in a bedsit in Belsize Park, near Camden. The whole band in one room! It was one of those big old houses in Belsize Park that were split into bedsits back then in the eighties, before London house prices went mental. It's probably a £3 million townhouse now or an overpriced boutique hotel, but back then it was a shithole. The whole band – me, our kid, Bez, Mark Day, Paul Davis and Gaz Whelan – were in one room that had six beds squeezed into it, and it wasn't as if it was a big room either. On the floor above us were six builders, all squeezed into one room, and then above them were six electricians, all squeezed into another room. We all had to share the same khazis and showers. Two khazis and two showers between eighteen blokes! You can imagine the state they were in. That was a bit of a comedown. You think you've made it, off to London to record your debut album with one of The Velvet Underground… then we get there and we're all in one room, having to share a bog with some Geordie builders. It felt more like *Auf Wiedersehen, Pet* than sex, drugs and rock'n'roll. Factory had packed us off to London and said, 'There's £80 each to last you two weeks.' I think my £80 lasted me an hour. Literally. It just went. It's £80, isn't it? Even then that wasn't a lot of dough.

The first time we went to New York, in 1987, Tony Wilson put us up in the Chelsea Hotel, because of the history of the place, which was a very Wilson thing to do. Patti Smith had lived there, and Wilson was a massive fan of Patti Smith and her album *Horses*, which John Cale had produced, which probably gave him the idea to get John Cale to produce our debut album. We knew that Sid Vicious and Nancy had lived at the Chelsea Hotel, and Nancy had been found stabbed to death in their bathroom, as that was only a few years before. We gave the janitor or the concierge or whoever it was $20 to let us see the room, but there was fuck all to see. I bet the cheeky bastard probably made $200 a week doing that, charging people $20 to see the room.

You could write a whole book about the Chelsea Hotel, and people have. Leonard Cohen had also lived there and met Janis Joplin in the elevator at 3 a.m. one night and took her back to his room, which is what his song 'Chelsea Hotel No.2' is about. Cohen later said, 'I came to New York and I was living at other hotels and I had heard about the Chelsea Hotel as being a place where I might meet people of my own kind. And I did. It was a grand, mad place. I love hotels to which, at 4 a.m., you can bring along a midget, a bear and four ladies, take them to your room and no one cares about it at all.' That used to be my idea of a great hotel as well, Leonard! Not any more. I prefer a comfy bed and a decent night's kip these days.

The Chelsea is also mentioned in Joni Mitchell's 'Chelsea Morning', Lou Reed's 'Chelsea Girl' and Jefferson Airplane's 'Third Week in Chelsea'. Madonna used to live there in her early days in New York, and after we'd stayed there she went back and did the photoshoot for her *Sex* book there. It had 400 rooms but only a few of them were hotel rooms you could actually book as a guest; the rest were full of people who lived there full time. Loads of literary types and artists had lived there, including Mark Twain, Charles Bukowski, William S. Burroughs and Jackson Pollock. I didn't know at the time that Arthur C. Clarke wrote *2001: A Space Odyssey* there, which was a great film, and Jack Kerouac wrote *On The Road* there. Arthur Miller moved into the Chelsea Hotel, after he divorced Marilyn Monroe, and stayed there six years. Old Arthur reckoned you could get high from marijuana smoke just by being in the elevator, and said, 'This hotel does not belong to America. There are no vacuum cleaners, no rules and no shame.' I couldn't agree more with Arthur. It did still have a bit of a vibe and an atmosphere when we stayed there, but it was a shithole, to be honest. There were no carpets on the floor, just lino. You know you're staying in a bit of a rum gaff when even the floors are wipe-clean, know what I mean? But then New York was still dodgy then. It was a few years before it got cleaned up. When I go back there now, New York is sanitized and nothing like it was back then. It's unrecognizable as the grimy, dangerous New York it used to be.

When we were in London, in the early days we used to stay at The Columbia, an old run-down gaff near Lancaster Gate that loads of bands used to stay in back in the day. It's been done up since, but it was pretty scruffy back in the day. Another shithole. Ask Oasis – they used to stay there all the time on their first tours, and even named a song on their debut album, *Definitely Maybe*, after it. Noddy Holder and Slade used to stay there a lot too, back in the day. Noddy stayed up drinking 'til dawn in the hotel bar one night, and when it got to 8 a.m., the barman shouted over to him, 'Mr Holder, it's 8 a.m., this is the wake up call you booked!'. Everyone from Iggy Pop to Amy Winehouse to Stereophonics used to stay there, and they prided themselves on their 'relaxed attitude to after-show antics'. Although they weren't quite relaxed enough for the Mondays' after-show antics, as we got barred after taking a big gang of people back there after the album launch for *Bummed*, back in 1988. We had the launch party at Dingwalls in Camden, where we played live. Everyone in the place that night was on E, and a few journalists and London types had their first taste of it that night, supplied by one of us or our lot, and they didn't know what had hit them. The review of the gig in the *NME* said 'they play like the Sistine Chapel ceiling: high, colourful and holy. But especially high.' It went on to describe Bez as having 'pupils dilated wide enough to drive a stretch limo through, and dances as if he's swimming in glue'. After our launch, we all went down to Paul Oakenfold's club night at Heaven, and then everyone came back to The Columbia where we were staying. Bringing half a munted crowd back from an acid house club was a bit too much even for them, and we got barred. Oh well. It was a good night. Oasis later got barred as well, after one of them – Bonehead, I think it was – threw a load of furniture out of the window and it landed on the hotel manager's car.

We also stayed at the Portobello Hotel later on, when we had more money. It's a small gaff in Notting Hill, what they call a 'boutique hotel' now. Damon Albarn used to work behind the bar there, before Blur took off, and he's got a few juicy stories to tell about the place that I can't repeat here. Johnny Depp and Kate Moss used to stay there as well. Bez ended up out with them one night and they were in some gaff and someone warned them there was a load of paparazzi outside. Bez told them, 'Don't worry, Johnny, I'll sort it!' but when he went out the door he was bombarded by this wall of photographers. He couldn't believe it. He was used to being photographed on a night out by the odd snapper, but he hadn't seen anything like the amount of paparazzi waiting for Johnny Depp and Kate Moss. The Portobello is also where Alice Cooper was staying when he asked room service for some white mice for his boa constrictor that he had in his room. The local pet shop sent them, apparently.

When the band first took off, I actually didn't have anywhere to live at the time, I was in between flats, so I ended up moving into the Britannia Hotel in Manchester. It just seemed easier to stay there than to bother finding a flat, because we were on the road quite a bit and if you've got a flat it needs looking after, doesn't it? The Britannia was right in town, so you could nip out and do a bit of shopping, and there was a bar right next to the hotel. Me and our tour manager Muzzer must have stayed there for at least seven or eight months. All the maids and cleaners at that time were young girls who were all on E and coke themselves, out raving their tits off every night. We used to leave Es and lines chopped out on the side for them so that they'd stay out of our business, and they would tidy our clothes and stuff for us in return.

We did have an incident at the Midland Hotel in Manchester, when we first sold out the G-Mex, which is opposite. We had 20,000 Mondays fans coming over the weekend and knew there would be trouble for the hotel if our fans booked in there or even got in the bar. The police were already on our case, blaming us, which did my head in a bit. I'm sure when Elvis was playing Vegas, if something was robbed from the casino next door, they didn't pull Elvis in for questioning. Anyway, we tried to warn the hotel, but they were like, 'Oh, don't worry, we've had Frank Zappa and The Who here. It will be fine!' And I'm like, 'No, you don't understand. Frank Zappa and The Who have got *nothing* on our lot!' The manager was a dick and he just kept saying things like, 'Oh, we've had Phil Collins and the Bee Gees and other huge pop stars staying here. Don't worry!' And I'm like, 'Nah, you don't understand, mate. Our fans are not like fucking Phil Collins fans or Bee Gees fans! You NEED to get extra security on that weekend, trust us.' But they just laughed at us... and what happened? The place got abso-fucking-lutely hammered. The place got robbed to fuck. Hundreds of fans got in and ran round causing chaos. The staff pulled the shutters down on the bar, but the crowd forced them up again and folk were just helping themselves. There were display cabinets in the foyer that got smashed and robbed. Then they tried to blame us afterwards. I was like, 'How is it our fault?! We tried to fucking warn you, but you wouldn't listen, you dicks!' We knew it would happen because that's just how Manchester was back then, but they wouldn't listen to us. That happened quite a bit. We would get the blame for things that our fans would do, as if we could control 20,000 Mondays fans who had descended on the city for a big night out!

But, like I mentioned before, we never smashed up a hotel because we didn't want to attract attention to ourselves – especially me personally, because I was always carrying heroin. I didn't want the hotel manager to call the cops and them find heroin and then I'd get banged up. So we tried to be quite careful in hotels. Even when we were smoking weed in a hotel, we would block the bottom of the hotel door with towels so the smell didn't get out down the corridor because the last thing we wanted was to bring things on top for ourselves.

When Black Grape was taking off, and I was doing a lot of press, I was spending a lot of time in London. I eventually got an apartment in Hampstead for a bit, but before then I used to stay at The Landmark hotel a lot, which is behind Marylebone station. Apparently, Kanye West and a lot of the big American rappers like staying there when they're in town, because they like big hotel rooms and The Landmark has got bigger rooms than a lot of the other hotels in London. When I was living there, I used to run into Chris Eubank a lot, as he was staying there. That was when he used to have that big lorry of his. Remember that daft lorry he always used to go about in? God knows where he parked it in central London. I got on all right with Eubank, and we used to have a few pints in the bar together. If you could have told us then that we'd both be on *Celebrity Gogglebox* twenty-five years later, I wouldn't have known what you were on about. Reality TV hadn't even been invented back then. *Big Brother* hadn't even started.

I had another incident at The Landmark, when I got a part in *The Avengers* movie and I was staying there while we were shooting. One night I had a cup of hot chocolate at the bar and then went to bed, but as soon as I got in my room it was like *The Exorcist*. I just projectile-vomited everywhere. I ran to the bathroom, spewing everywhere, and got to the bathroom and projectile-vomited all over there as well. I cleaned up as much as I could, but I had a call at 5 a.m., with a car picking me up to be on set for 6 a.m., and I forgot to put the 'Do Not Disturb' sign on my room, so I could finish cleaning it up when I got back. Anyway, I didn't get back until 10 p.m. that night, and as I got out of the car the concierge said to me, quite aggressively, 'You fucking dirty bastard.' I was like 'You what?' because he'd been really nice to me the whole time I was staying there. But he was effing and jeffing at me, saying, 'You dirty bastard, shitting yourself all over your room...' and I was like, 'Wooooahhh! Hold on a fucking minute!' So the concierge and me went up to my room and I think a couple of people from housekeeping were there too, because the maid who discovered it had proper freaked out and refused to clean it up. Madness. Anyway, they put me down in the hotel's incident book. They weren't having it, that it was hot chocolate. I was like, 'Scoop some of it up and send it away for testing, it's fucking hot chocolate!' So obviously I stopped staying at The Landmark after that.

These days, I appreciate a decent hotel, and there's no partying in the hotel bar until the early hours. I try and get home as much as I can after a day's work. Even if I'm down in London doing press or TV, I'll try and get back home if I can. But if I'm on tour or staying down in London, I'll usually stay in a nice gaff like a Hilton or something like that. I'll probably just be chilling after a long day. I'm more likely to be found watching the Discovery channel in my room than downstairs in the bar, trying to discover where the party is at.

# Homes

For some reason, a lot of people seem to think I still live next door to Bez. That we're neighbours and have some sort of *Stella Street* thing going on. I did live next door to him for a little while in Hadfield, just outside Glossop, but that was nearly twenty years ago now. I had nowhere to live at the time, and this little cottage backing on to Bez's came up for rent so I moved there. For some reason, the idea that me and Bez are neighbours amused some people and it was just one of those things that stuck. I don't know if they had a romanticized idea of me and Bez being neighbours and popping round to borrow a packet of skins or something. Hadfield is also where they filmed *The League of Gentlemen*, so the idea of me and Bez living there obviously greatly amused some people.

The one time me and Bez did live together was carnage. As you might expect. I had a gaff in Boothstown in Salford in the mid-eighties with my then girlfriend, and then when we split up she moved out and our Paul and Bez moved in. Not long after they moved in, we had to break in one night, as we all forgot our keys, and we never bothered to get the front door fixed, so it was like an open house and anyone could just walk in off the street. We used to have all these madheads turning up at all hours of the day and night. I also used it as a stash house, as I was selling drugs at the time, so had all sorts hidden in the loft. The song 'Moving In With' from *Bummed* is all about that gaff. 'You've got two bent pigs in the crash downstairs below' – that was about two bent coppers who we used to serve up. They would buy all sorts from us – speed, weed and even smack. They would pull up outside in their police car to buy it off us. Mental. The 'schizophrenic acquaintance patient with no place to go' was a huge kid called Paul who was one of the many madheads who used to come round all the time. He'd been sectioned but he'd been released and used to come round in these huge African gowns with a kitten on each shoulder. No shit, a live kitten on each shoulder. We had to tell him to stop coming round after he started intimidating people. It was a mad gaff, that, looking back. You had to hide anything you had when you were living there – drugs, money, even your bloody clothes – or they would all be gone when you woke up. It was first up, best dressed. If I slept in, I'd wake up and find that Bez or our Paul was already wearing my clothes. That's what the line in 'Performance' that says 'I took to hiding, I took to hiding, hiding strange things' is about.

There's a hotel near where I live now, in Salford, where I do a lot of my interviews and filming, so it's dead handy. It's also near to my mam and, as my dad passed away recently and our Paul is based in the States, I was glad to be near her when lockdown happened, so I could drop off some shopping and stuff for her. It was weird having to leave stuff on the doorstep and keep your distance. I went to give her a kiss and a hug as I was leaving some stuff for her once, without thinking, and then I thought, 'Shit! Have I just killed my mum?' because I knew I had more chance of catching it than other people, because of my medical history.

I've done a few collaborations during lockdown and I can do those in my home studio. Whoever I'm working with just sends me the track or the beats, and I then record my vocals in the home studio and send it back to them. One of our kids, Oli, is in his early twenties and is a DJ and knows what he is doing in the studio, so he can help me record the vocals and send them to whoever I'm working with.

I quite like chilling out at home these days. Seriously. I love washing up. I never used to. When me, Bez and our Paul shared that flat in Salford, the washing-up would never ever get done, and it got to the stage once where the pile of pots was so big, after weeks and weeks, that we ended up having to do the washing-up in the bath. It took me fifty years to discover that washing up is really relaxing, and I now do all the washing-up when I'm at home. There's something about getting shit off plates and cutlery. My mind goes completely blank and I love it. I don't use the dishwasher, I actually do them by hand. You know where you are with washing-up.

# The recording studio

The first time we ever went into a recording studio was with Mike Pickering, who later went on to have huge success with M People. I think it was the first time Mike had recorded a band other than his own band that he had at the time, Quando Quango. We didn't have any idea how the recording process worked and I really don't think we were ready to get put down on tape. I think you can tell that, listening to the recording. I was disappointed when I heard the recordings because I was hoping it would sound a bit more like Quando Quango, because I quite liked them. When I get the sense that something's not right I can be quite difficult if I don't want to be there, and I maybe was with Mike. A bit like *Yes Please!* years later.

I just think we weren't ready, and it's a shame because Mike was really into us as a band and he 'got' us more than the other people on Factory. The timing was just wrong. We did three tracks with him – 'Delightful', This Feeling' and

'Oasis', which came out as the *Forty Five* EP. I don't think any of the band really like 'This Feeling'. We thought it sounded too twee and indie, too much like these wishy-washy indie bands who were trying to copy Orange Juice or whoever, and that's not what we were after. It's too fast as well. We were quite nervous then and the band would play too fast, though we'd probably had a bit of speed as well. It was similar when we went into Strawberry Studios with Bernard Sumner for the next single. We just weren't ready really.

When it came to recording our debut album, Wilson picked John Cale and sent us down to the Firehouse Studio in London. I can't remember much about that actual studio – it was pretty nondescript – and it was a very straight recording. Cale basically had us playing the songs live.

In the studio it's about chemistry more than anything – George Martin had never recorded rock'n'roll before The Beatles but he was perfect for them. We never really had a fight in the studio when we were recording. With the Mondays, if we all fell out we'd just all fuck off and not bother turning up. Or I certainly would. For the first three albums there was no huge falling-out. It was when the egos came out to play that things went tits up, for the fourth album, but even then there was no fighting in the studio. I was hardly there, for a start. I was so not into what they were doing that I just wouldn't show up.

But loads of bands have really come to blows in the studio. Captain Beefheart pulled a crossbow on one member of his band. It never got that bad with the Mondays. Noel and Liam had a huge fight when they were recording their second album, *(What's The Story) Morning Glory*, in Rockfield.

Liam had been down the pub and brought a load of locals back to the studio. I wouldn't have been into that. That's the sort of thing Bez would do. Anyway, Noel and Liam had a huge bust-up and Noel ended up whacking Liam with a cricket bat. The whole place got trashed and Noel fucked off to London, and Liam went home to his mam Peggy's in Manchester with his leg in plaster and she was like, 'What kind of record have you been making down there?'

I've also recorded in Rockfield – we recorded the first Black Grape album there. It's a mad studio in a converted farmhouse in Wales owned by two brothers. Black Sabbath and Hawkwind used to record there back in the day. The Stone Roses were there, recording *Second Coming*, when we were there. The Charlatans and Manic Street Preachers have also recorded there, and Coldplay did their first album. A documentary film just came out about it called *Rockfield: The Studio on the Farm*. It's quite a magical place, really. You're cut off from reality down there. Maybe that's why the Roses spent forever making that second album.

You can lose all sense of space and time in the studio if you're not careful. Especially if drugs are involved. I've had good and bad experiences around recording studios with drugs. *Bummed* was totally made on ecstasy, and it worked because it locked us in to a groove. But that's not always the case. Obviously crack cocaine had a really detrimental effect on the recording of *Yes Please!*, although I don't think anyone would really think it would have any other effect. Cocaine can be really bad as well, as it distorts your mindset and you're full of yourself and think whatever you're recording is fucking incredible. Oasis went through that and Noel himself said, 'There's times when you're recording and you're listening back to what you've just recorded, and you want to eat yourself because it's so incredible... and then you get up in the morning and it sounds like *Trumpton*! If you can record music when you're straight that gets you off when you're high, then you've smashed it. It's very rare that it happens the other way round, or is for this band anyway.'

But that's Oasis, and every band's different. It's all about creating the right vibe in the studio, and drugs are just one part of that mix. When The Beatles were in Abbey Road, they used to sneak off and have a spliff when they thought George Martin wasn't watching. With Black Sabbath, Tony Iommi said, 'We were getting really drugged out, doing a lot of dope. We'd go down to the sessions, and have to pack up because we were too stoned, we'd have to stop. Nobody could get anything right, we were all over the place, everybody's playing a different thing. We'd go back and sleep it off, and try again the next day.'

For our second album, it was decided we would record it in an old abattoir in Driffield in East Yorkshire. I know, doesn't sound rock'n'roll, does it? But it's true. The studio was called Slaughterhouse (I know) and it was literally an old abattoir that had been converted into a studio, but they'd done a decent job of converting it. An abattoir. I think it's a safe bet Morrissey has never recorded there. I can't remember who chose Driffield, but it was probably Martin Hannett. I'd never heard of Driffield before. It had been used by goth-type bands and Yorkshire bands like The Sisters of Mercy – there was quite a big goth thing going on over that side of the

Pennines in the eighties – but no one like us. The studio was a weird set-up. As well as being an old abattoir, there was a little cobbled street and a telephone box actually inside the building. Our Paul and Martin Hannett managed to get locked in the studio one night, when they were on acid, and it completely did their heads in. They thought they were outside and were trying to work our which way down the street the pub was, for about an hour.

Those few weeks in Driffield were bananas. We were totally on our own E vibe at the time and, although the E culture was taking off in Manchester, it had yet to hit little places like Driffield. The locals had no idea what to make of us. They would just be staring at us. Our whole behaviour and the way we looked, with our designer hippy gear thing going on, was totally alien to them. A year later, half the kids in Driffield had probably got on it but, at the time, it was still this little backwards Yorkshire place, and we were totally on one. We were off our tits, acting like cartoon characters. We'd walk down the high street or into a shop, doing that mad little walk that Madness used to do. That thing they did in their videos, where they're all marching in unison? We'd walk in a shop like that to get some rizlas or something and the old dears wouldn't know what to make of us. We'd be dancing down the high street and across zebra crossings, off our tits. Tony Wilson was keen to know how recording was going, so he drove over from Manchester one night. He said he arrived and walked into the studio and it was completely dark, with bodies lying all over the floor, surrounded by 12" records, and acid house banging out in the dark.

The next studio we used was a step up again: Richard Branson's The Manor in Oxford, which was one of the first residential studios in the UK. One of the first albums recorded there was *Tubular Bells* by Mike Oldfield, which went on to sell millions and basically funded the growth of Virgin. The studio was then used for loads of Virgin acts, and everyone from Queen to INXS had recorded there. It was great for us, we were buzzing off being in this big old country house. We were down there to record songs for what became the *Madchester Rave On* EP featuring 'Hallelujah' and 'Rave On'. We had already written the songs before we went into the studio and they were probably the first songs that had been influenced right from the very start by the whole E scene. My memory is a bit hazy of the recording there, as we were pretty off it at the time. So was Hannett. He wasn't in great shape then, doing a lot of drugs, and he would literally pass out on the mixing desk and be passed out all day. At the same time we were down there recording with Hannett, Branson was hosting one of his hot-air balloon parties there. He was on his balloon vibe at the time, trying to break some record, and he had this garden party with all the 'great and good' there, loads of celebs and even some royalty. One of those sorts of parties where fucking everyone turns up. A proper circus. For once, even the Mondays were on quite good behaviour and didn't cause a scene.

When it came to our third album, *Pills 'n' Thrills and Bellyaches*, we'd made it. We'd made the jump to *Top of the Pops* and playing Wembley Arena, so Factory were prepared to spend a bit more money on recording the album, and we ended up recording at the famous Capitol

Studios in Los Angeles. Which was a bit of a jump from the last album, from an old abattoir in Driffield to The Beach Boys' iconic old studio in LA, know what I mean? That was such a buzz for us. We knew all the records that had been recorded there, the sun was shining, it was just a great buzz, and great to be out of Manchester for a while. That may sound like a crazy thing to say because Manchester and Madchester were all over the press and everyone else thought it was the centre of the world, but we were a bit ahead of the curve and it had started to get a bit much. Manchester can get quite claustrophobic and it had all got a bit on top. At the time, both us and the Roses were getting a bit bored with the 'Madchester' tag. We certainly never wanted to just be a local band, we wanted to appeal to everyone. Ian Brown said to Tony Wilson at the time, when Wilson kept talking about Madchester, 'It's not right, this – it excludes everyone else outside the Manchester postcode. It's like saying we are cool and they are not.' A few years later, Ian was doing a documentary with Wilson and he admitted to Ian, 'You know, you were right. We shouldn't have done that. The Mondays never wanted to do that Madchester thing and we made them do it.'

Capitol Studios are on Hollywood and Vine, near Sunset Strip, so it's right bang in the middle of proper LA. It's an iconic round building and a famous Hollywood landmark. Frank Sinatra was one of the first artists to record there, when it was built in 1956, then everyone from Nat King Cole to The Beach Boys used it. The Beastie Boys had released *Paul's Boutique* the year before we were there, and they flew their flag from the top of the studio, although they'd mostly recorded it in home studios with Dust Brothers.

We were only supposed to have a week in there at the start, but it was going so great, we persuaded the record label to let us do a whole month. The sunshine definitely helped the vibe, it's a sunshiny album. If *Bummed* is more claustrophobic, recorded in a Yorkshire abattoir on ecstasy, *Pills 'n' Thrills* is the sound of us in LA, chilled out on strong California weed, with the sun on our faces. Oakenfold had his decks set up in the studio, and we were vibing off his records, and he'd play something that was in the mood of the song we were recording and that would be inspire us. Gaz played the drums on 'God's Cop', playing along to Oakey DJing. We might have been tagged in back home with the Madchester thing or baggy thing – both titles I hated – but that didn't bear any relation to the music that we were inspired by and the record we wanted to make. On the one hand, we were listening to classic stuff like Stevie Wonder and Chic, and on the other we had the Balearic influence of the clubs we were going to, that Ibiza influence, and obviously that's where Oakenfold was coming from as well.

Lots of people said we were one of the first bands to bring an acid house influence to rock'n'roll, but it was more of that Balearic end of acid house rather than the squelchy acid sound. It became a cliché to say there's always been a dance element to our music, when every fucker like the Soup Dragons jumped on the bandwagon and started doing dance remixes of their tunes, but that element *was* always there in our music. Listen back to the early Mondays stuff, and there was undeniably always a groove there. It's just that, after ecstasy and being exposed to those Balearic records and acid house, it came more to the front.

Factory hadn't heard anything, and Wilson flew out to Los Angeles halfway through recording. He was probably a bit worried that we were running up a big studio bill while just partying, rather than recording. But the first thing we played him was 'Bob's Yer Uncle' and he was blown away. I think hearing that was payback for him, after years of telling everyone how great the Mondays were. That's what he said, anyway. He later told the press: 'It was a real golden moment. I think I knew from then on that this would be one of the great Factory albums, actually one of the great British albums of the age.' Typical Wilson. But you know, he was right. When he died seventeen years later, in 2007, 'Bob's Yer Uncle' was one of two songs he asked to be played at his funeral, along with 'Atmosphere' by Joy Division.

I've got a studio at home now, so I've been doing a lot of recording at home during lockdown. I've done a track with Robbie Williams, and a track with Noel Gallagher. They send me the track or the beats or whatever, and I just record my vocals here and send them back. The Robbie one is supposed to be coming out soon. Alan is just now sorting out the bits and bobs. Watch this space!

# Producers

I think it takes most bands a while to realize what the role of the producer is, and what sort of producer they work best with. I've been lucky to work with some of the most famous and brilliant producers in music in my time, although what looks great on paper doesn't always work brilliantly in the studio in real life. A lot of it is about chemistry, and I don't mean that sort of chemistry.

With Happy Mondays, our run of producers from the start was ridiculous: Mike Pickering (Haçienda/M People), Bernard Sumner (Joy Division/New Order/Electronic), John Cale (The Velvet Underground), Martin Hannett (Joy Division/Factory), Paul Oakenfold and Steve Osborne, Tina Weymouth and Chris Frantz (Talking Heads). It's a ridiculous run of producers really, although some of the sessions worked out better than others.

The first producer we ever worked with was Mike Pickering, who did really get the Mondays and where we were coming from, but I just don't think we were ready as a band to get in the studio at that stage. That recording session didn't really work for me, but it wasn't Mike's fault. We still didn't have a clue how the recording process worked or what the role of a producer was. We just thought they were there to record you playing your songs. We didn't have a clue how the recording studio could actually be used as an instrument. If you'd shown me a mixing desk back then, I'd probably have thought it was something you cut sheet metal on. We were clueless. I'll admit I was probably a bit difficult as well, as I can be when I sense that things aren't going well, which is what happened to a much worse degree later, when we worked with Chris and Tina from Talking Heads on *Yes Please!*

The second time we went into the studio it was with Bernard Sumner as producer. Like everyone, we were huge fans of Joy Division and New Order, and we'd already supported New Order on tour. I was also a big fan of Bernard Sumner's production work, especially 'Reach For Love' by Marcel King, which he produced with Donald Johnson from A Certain Ratio as Be Productions. ACR had one of the rehearsal rooms next to us under the Boardwalk, and we'd seen Donald messing around with samplers and stuff. Marcel had been the lead singer in Sweet Sensation when he was a kid in the seventies, and they had a No.1 hit with 'Sad Sweet Dreamer' when he was still only seventeen. 'Reach For Love' is a total lost classic in my book (and this *is* my book). It's probably my favourite single that Factory ever released, but it sank without trace, which was a real shame. Marcel ended up homeless, sleeping rough in his car in Moss Side, and died of a brain haemorrhage in 1995, poor bloke. When we recorded the second Black Grape album, just after he died, I suggested to Kermit that we add a bit on 'Get Higher' so people might go back and rediscover it, but I don't think many did. If you haven't heard it, stick it on now, it's a top track that everyone should know.

Before we went into the studio with Bernard, Vini Reilly from Durutti Column had been suggested as a producer, but he only lasted about two hours in the room with us before he decided he couldn't handle us, which didn't surprise me one bit. I like Vini and everyone knows he's a genius guitar player, but he's always been a very fragile individual. Vini once told everyone I'd spiked him one night at the Haçienda, and the next morning I had Tony Wilson and everyone on the phone, getting on my case, saying, 'Shaun, why the fuck did you do that to poor Vini? You know what he's like.' I was like, 'What the fuck are you on about? I didn't spike anyone. It's all in his mind.' I was never one for spiking anyone, that's just a waste of good drugs. Anyway, fuck knows who thought he would be a good match for a bunch of unruly scallies like us – probably Wilson, as he'd always been the biggest champion of Vini – but it didn't end up happening and we went into the studio with Bernard.

We still probably weren't ready to be in the studio as a band at that stage, but it was a much better session. Bernard managed to capture that looser, spacey dance element of the Mondays that we hadn't managed to get on tape in the earlier sessions. He also kept in a snippet of me getting at the band, shouting 'Shut up, Gaz, we're starting,' and then, 'Ronnie!' which is what we used to call him, after Ronnie Whelan, the

Liverpool player. That was what our early gigs and recording sessions were like: 'Right, are you ready or what?'

The end result, the single 'Freaky Dancin'', was much better than our session with Mike Pickering, but I knew we still hadn't nailed it and we could do much better. That recording session with Bernard is probably most famous for me and Bez fishing Bernard's Chinese takeaway out of the bin and eating the leftovers. As I mentioned earlier, that story is true but it does get slightly exaggerated, like everything.

When we came to record our debut album, Factory put us together with John Cale from The Velvet Underground. Cale had already produced three classic debut albums, by The Stooges, Modern Lovers and Patti Smith, and Wilson was a huge fan of Patti Smith's album *Horses*. Cale had been on Wilson's Granada TV show, *So It Goes*, and also appeared at Festival of the Tenth Summer. Obviously we were all Velvet Underground fans, and I think Wilson thought it would work and be a great press story about Happy Mondays working with a Velvet Underground producer. Apparently, when Wilson first asked John Cale to produce us, Cale asked him what we were like, and Wilson said, 'The best way I can describe them, so you know what you're letting yourself in for, John, is scum. They are fucking scum.' Cheeky bastard. But with Tony, that was meant as compliment in his eyes.

What we didn't know was that Cale had just gone straight, after years of struggling with drug and alcohol issues. So he turned up at the studio on the first day with this box of tangerines and a bag of Extra Strong Mints. That was his way of staying off the gear. He'd work his way through the tangerines and mints while we were in the studio, and as soon as he'd finished them he was off, that was him done for the day. So that was a bit of a bad mix, as we were just getting started on our drug-taking, while he was retiring from his! He was a bit stand-offish and maybe we were a little bit in awe of him because he'd been in The Velvet Underground and we were still new to the studio, you know? We still didn't know our way round the studio or the recording process, and the only people we'd been in the studio with at that stage were Mike and Bernard, who we knew pretty well. We'd never been in the studio with someone we didn't know.

Even though he'd created all this leftfield music with the Velvets, John was a classically trained musician, so he came at music from a totally different angle from us, who weren't trained at all. He'd made all this avant-garde music, but I don't think he'd ever come across anything like us. I remember he was really intrigued by Mark Day's unusual way of guitar playing, and he said to him, 'Where did you get those chords from?' and Mark went, 'I think I got them from Marks & Spencer.' Mark wasn't even joking! We were like, 'He means your guitar chords, you tit, not your trousers!'

Working with Martin Hannett, on our second album, was the opposite of working with John Cale. I'd never met Hannett before the recording. He was a bit of a mystery character. He'd made his name producing Joy Division, and really helped create a unique sound for them, but then he'd fallen out with Factory and gone off the rails a bit. I'd sung about him on 'Tart Tart' – 'Martin sleeps on the desk/He wears a sleeping bag for his vest' – but I'd never actually met him at that stage. That was just a snippet based on what Bernard Sumner had told me about working with him. When we were recording our debut album, Cale had always been egging the band on to play faster, but Hannett wanted us to play 'slower but faster'. That's what he was like.

Working with Hannett was the first time we experienced using the studio as an instrument, that it wasn't just about recording you playing your songs, that you could actually use the studio to take your songs somewhere else.

After *Bummed*, when acid house was taking off, it had been my idea to bring the DJ Paul Oakenfold in to do a remix of 'Wrote For Luck', and that worked out so well that I was really keen to work with him on our third album. No one had thought of working with a DJ in the studio at that time, really. Even Factory were a bit unsure at first (and they owned the bloody Haçienda so should have known what DJs were capable of!) but, after the remix worked really well, they were up for it. I just thought that the Balearic influence Oakenfold could bring would work really well with the groove of the Mondays. He brought Osborne with him, as Oakey had never really been in a studio before so needed someone who could engineer it and do all the technical stuff that he was just still learning really. How we worked with Oakey was a new way of working and it was great for us. He'd DJ and come up with beats in the studio and the band jammed alongside him. The album was a knockout and look where Oakey is now. We were the first ones to bring him into the studio and now he's this superstar producer and DJ, playing stadiums and worth millions.

The last Happy Mondays album we did, with Tina Weymouth and Chris Frantz from Talking Heads, wasn't a success but that wasn't necessarily their fault. The band was already fracturing before we arrived in Barbados, and we didn't really have any music ready. I liked Talking Heads, and who knows what would have happened if we'd recorded with them at another time, but I think *Yes Please!* was pretty much doomed from the start. The first day I went into the studio I just wasn't vibing off what I was hearing. Everyone in the band wanted to show off what they were capable of, rather than doing what they had done on previous records, which was all working to the benefit of the tune, rather than themselves. I really don't think Chris and Tina knew what they were letting themselves in for. If you want to judge how the mood in the Mondays had changed, just look at the mood and the lyrics of the closing song on *Pills 'n' Thrills* and the opening track on *Yes Please!* Where *Pills 'n' Thrills* closes with 'Harmony' – an upbeat, euphoric, sunny song with me on top of the world, singing 'I'd like to teach the world to sing in perfect harmony' – the opening track of *Yes Please!* is the downbeat, darker beats of 'Stinkin' Thinkin'', and I sound exhausted, whispering 'I'm tied down with stinkin' thinkin'/Stinkin' thinkin' gets you nowhere'. I mean, the change in mood couldn't be more striking. Everything had got a bit dark.

After the nightmare of *Yes Please!*, recording with Danny Saber for the first Black Grape album, *It's Great When You're Straight... Yeah*, was a real breath of fresh air. As I've mentioned before, I really wanted the first Black Grape album to be a cross between the more upbeat end of the Rolling Stones and Cypress Hill, so Danny was perfect, as he'd done the beats for Cypress Hill and he can also play a few instruments. Danny also works really fast, which is great for me. Back then I hadn't been diagnosed with ADHD but I've never had a huge attention span, so when I'm recording I prefer to keep momentum up and bounce fresh ideas off the tunes. As soon as things start to get bogged down a bit I start to lose interest.

After the Mondays got back together, we decided to do a new album in 2006, and Elliot Rashman, who was managing us then, suggested we bring in Sunny Levine as producer. Sunny is the grandson of Quincy Jones, which means he's pretty much royalty when it comes to production. When he was a kid, his granddad was producing the *Thriller* and *Bad* albums for Michael Jackson, you know what I mean? It doesn't get any bigger than that. Sunny lived with his mum near the studio in LA and would pop into the studio after school sometimes to see his grandad while he was recording *Bad* with Michael Jackson!

Sunny had then worked in studios since he was a kid himself. He started as a tea boy and worked his way up. Elliot had known Sunny since he was a kid, because his dad, Stewart Levine (Quincy Jones' son), was also a producer and had worked on most of the Simply Red albums – and Elliot used to manage Simply Red. Sunny had grown up in that great production family, and Elliot knew that the two of us would be able to work well together. Sunny was great. I found it really easy to work with him. He came over to Manchester and we worked at Moolah Rouge studios in Stockport at first, then we went over and finished the album at Sunny's studio in Venice Beach in LA. I think we nailed the whole thing in about two weeks. We even had a couple of secret guests on there, including Ry Cooder and his son Joachim, who is a drummer and best mates with Sunny. We didn't exploit the fact that they were guests on the record at the time, because they were simply mates of Sunny's who did it as a favour to him. I don't think the record company even knew Ry Cooder was on the album.

Because we nailed it really quickly, and I really liked working with Sunny, I was keen to work with him again after that and did a solo album with him called *Visits From Future Technology*, which only came out in the summer of 2021. In my delusional ADHD brain, it's my *Sgt Pepper's*, full of different-flavoured songs. We put a couple of tracks on Spotify a couple of years ago and one track 'Close The Dam' got over a million hits. I'm not even sure how that took off, but it did. It went viral or whatever you call it, and next thing a million people have got on it.

We also did a new Black Grape album in 2017, and for that we brought in Youth as a producer. Youth was one of the founding members of Killing Joke but has been a producer for the last thirty years and has worked with everyone from The Orb to Take That. He's also behind a few records that some people don't really know are him, like that Blue Pearl record 'Naked in the Rain' that was a huge hit back in 1990. Youth is just insanely good at making really great pop records. He's so versatile. I loved that remix he did of Edwyn Collins' 'A Girl Like You' too. I just thought if we mixed that pop sensibility with me and Kermit and all our wacky references and cartoon imagery it could be a perfect recipe. Youth's great at working quickly, and with *Pop Voodoo* we had the whole thing written, recorded and produced in four weeks. You can really trust Youth. He works on instinct and – unlike most producers – doesn't continually insist on changing shit around that is already good. Like the opening track, 'Everything You Know Is Wrong'. A lot of that track was down to Youth. He secretly recorded me and Kermit chatting about Trump and American politics. Like a lot of people when Trump was in power, we were feeling pretty paranoid about what he was going to do. The next thing me and Kermit know, Youth plays us what's he got and *boom*, there's a beat on it, and then *boomph*, there's some bass on it, so he built it up from there and turned it into a track. It was totally spontaneous and most of it's just stream-of-consciousness rambling. It's meant to be like a skit on a hip-hop album where it's an introduction to the record as a whole, and I think it works well. *Pop Voodoo* was the logical extension of *It's Great When You're Straight… Yeah* to me. It's the album we should really have made next. Just like *It's Great When You're Straight* is actually the album the Mondays could have made after *Pills 'n' Thrills*.

There might have been a long gap, but we were well conscious we wanted to make something that was obviously a Black Grape record, but not something that still sounded like the nineties. We went into the studio with the idea we wanted to mix The Beach Boys, The Beatles and Geto Boys with a bit of *Scarface*, you know? We had all these ideas, but we also wanted something timeless, something that sounds right in the *now*, and Youth totally got it. I'd happily work with Youth again, as he's great, he totally gets how I like working.

The best advice I'd give on finding the right producer is: find someone you get on with, someone who's on your wavelength, and someone who works at the right pace for you. A lot of it is chemistry and you won't know until you get in the studio together. Looking back, I think I've been really lucky with the run of producers I've had. A lot of them are legendary names, and were far more experienced than we were when we worked with them, but thankfully most of them got the Mondays or Black Grape.

# Singles

Nowadays, with most people streaming music in some way or another, there's less emphasis on singles than there was back in the day. Thirty years ago, the single was your biggest chance of getting someone's attention, and hopefully getting them interested in the album that was following. Back in 1990, you'd regularly get singles that sold over a million, which seems mental now, considering that nowadays you can get in the charts by only selling a few thousand.

Singles usually get decided by the band and management, with the record company. At most record companies, the A&R guy might have quite a big say in it, and maybe even the deciding vote. But Factory was different, they generally just let us pick what tracks we wanted as singles. Wilson did push for the *Madchester Rave On* EP to be called that, which I was against, but I think that's the only real time that Factory pushed us to do something that wasn't our choice.

Our first single should have been 'Tart Tart' really. The two that came before that – *Forty Five* EP and 'Freaky Dancin'' – you can tell we were still finding our feet really, and those singles should never have seen the light of day, in my book. 'Tart Tart' was the first time I felt we'd really nailed our sound on a single, and the biggest buzz for us with that single was getting the video shown on *The Chart Show*. That felt like a buzz, and it got to No.13 in the indie charts. The next single was '24 Hour Party People', which felt like a step up again, and felt like a proper single that would get radio play and get played at clubs. 'Lazyitis' was a bit of a curveball – it was another of our takes on country and western, after 'Country Song' (which was originally called 'Some Cunt From Preston', our nickname for country and western). I wasn't that happy with the album version. I didn't think we quite nailed it, but Wilson insisted he wanted it to be a single and to bring in Karl Denver, who was famous for his hit single 'Wimoweh'. I wasn't quite sure, but it worked out to be this great off-the-wall pop single. This was the video we shot under the Mancunian Way where we were all dressed as convicts. Quite ironic, really, considering I actually got nicked and slung in prison while I was promoting it. I had to go and meet Karl Denver in Jersey to do some press, as Karl was doing a season of gigs out there. We'd played in London the night before and I was a bit the worse for wear and got stopped by customs at Jersey. They didn't know who I was, they just thought I was some scally. They searched my bags and found some little bags that had traces of coke on them and locked me up. The prison in Jersey was unreal, I've never seen a prison like it. It looked like the prison in *Midnight*

*Express* or something. It was medieval. I was shackled up by the ankle to the fucking chain gang with ten other blokes like *The Shawshank Redemption* or something. We all had to shuffle around together and go for a piss together. It was barbaric. Tony Wilson had to come over and sort it, and the only reason they gave me bail was because I was playing a benefit gig for Hillsborough with the Mondays. The myth about that incident was Tony came to see me in my cell and said, 'You need an advocate,' and I said, 'I don't need any poncy Southern drink, Tony. I'm in the shit here, just get me out of here!' But take that with a pinch of salt. I knew what a bloody advocate was by then.

The next single was the one that really changed things for us. The acid house scene was really taking off and I was really into Paul Oakenfold's 'Jibaro' so I suggested we get him in to remix 'Wrote For Luck'. There was no established culture of getting DJs to remix songs by bands, but I knew it could work. I didn't know if it *would*, but I knew if Oakey got it right it would cross over on the dancefloors. Factory went for it, thankfully, and also got Vince Clarke from Erasure to remix it (I think they wanted a bigger name as no one knew who Oakenfold was back then, apart from a few acid house heads). Both remixes were great, although I preferred Oakey's 'WFL (Think About The Future)' and it really helped cement our place at the forefront of the whole scene. It got to No.3 in the indie charts and I could feel that we were really on our way then, it felt like we were riding a wave.

The next single became the *Madchester Rave On* EP. One of the Bailey brothers came up with 'Madchester' because it did feel mad in Manchester at that time, but I thought it was a bit corny. Wilson loved it, though. He thought the press would jump on it, and he was right on that score. After the success of the remixes of 'WFL', I think he could sense that all of a sudden the Mondays were about to break through. We got Oakenfold in to do remixes again, along with Andrew Weatherall and Terry Farley from Boys Own, and released two different versions of the EP and that's when everything went mental. It was getting loads of airplay and it went to No.1 in the indie chats and No.19 in the main charts, and all of a sudden we were on *Top of the Pops*. That was our breakthrough moment, and we suddenly jumped from playing 200- or 300-capacity venues to playing to 20,000 people over a weekend at G-Mex in Manchester. From then on it just felt like a rollercoaster with no brakes.

Compared to the previous two singles, where we knew exactly what we wanted, our next single happened by accident really, and it went on to be our huge breakthrough hit. Although we were on Factory in the UK, we were signed to Elektra in the States, and at the start of 1990 it was their fortieth anniversary and they decided they wanted to do a compilation with all their current bands doing covers of songs from their back catalogue. I wasn't really arsed about doing it, so when they sent us this tape over we listened to it and the first or second song was 'Step On' by John Kongos. I'd never heard it before, but straight away I could hear us playing our own version of it, and I'd knew it would be quite easy to rip it and add our own thing to it. The Mondays version is quite different to the original.

I'd always been a fan of Steve McQueen, and not long before we were due to record 'Step On', I'd watched this great documentary on him, called *Man On The Edge*. There was this really old-school, big-time film producer in it, talking about when he met McQueen for the first time, and he said, 'This cool kid came in, and I could tell he was an actor. He said to me, "You can't tell me what's what, man! You're twisting my melon, man!"' He was a pretty feisty bloke, McQueen. Then this producer said, 'This kid talked so hip!' Straight away, those two lines hit me, as I was watching the film. I just thought, 'That's fucking great, I'm having that!' and started rolling it round in my head and making it my own. I think some people from down south or abroad thought it was a Manc saying, that we were all walking round, tripping, going 'You're twisting my melon, man,' but it wasn't. I just lifted it from that McQueen doc. He was a cool fucker. He was an orphan who lied about his age when he was fifteen, to join the marines, then got into acting because he thought it would be a great way to attract women. He was cool as fuck and had a great haircut and wore really cool clothes. He was only about five foot eight or something, but he was a proper handy little fucker as well. It makes me laugh when people wank on about James Dean. Please. James Dean wasn't even in the same league as Steve McQueen – *nowhere near* the same league. McQueen was the original casual, the original Perry Boy.

The other catchphrase in 'Step On' came from one of our mates in the Haçienda, Bobby Gillette, who was always shouting, 'Call the cops!' He'd stand in the middle of the club, off his nut, whistling and shouting, 'Call the cops! … We're here! The Mancs! Our firm! Our corner! … CALL THE COPS!'

It was a proper magpie approach. I just took those two elements, stuck them together, and came up with: 'You're twisting my melon, man/You talk so hip, you know you're twisting my melon, man/Call the cops!' That's exactly what I thought 'Step On' needed. It was really simple to record. The band laid down their parts and then I went in to do my vocals and I played around with the phrasing of the lyrics and added all my new bits. The producers, Paul Oakenfold and Steve Osborne, got to grips with it and added that huge booming bottom end and it was really beginning to sound mega. But I still thought there was something missing from it. I thought I could hear a gospel backing vocal on it, which is not the first thing you'd expect on a Mondays track back then. But I mentioned that to our manager Nathan, and he'd been approached by a singer called Rowetta in the Haçienda, who said, 'You manage Happy Mondays, don't you? I fucking love that band!' She was managed by Elliot Rashman, so Nathan gave him a call and Rowetta came down and added a simple backing vocal, which was the final touch it needed. Rowetta ended up joining the band, and she's still with us today, thirty years later.

When I heard the finished track, I was like, 'This is too good to give to that compilation. This is the single we need to get us back in the charts, before the album.' We needed a single to release to tide us over until the next album – what would become *Pills 'n' Thrills* – and 'Step On' was perfect. We still had to give a track to Elektra, so we went back and listened to the tape they'd sent us, and the next song on there was 'Tokoloshe Man', also by John Kongos, so we just bashed that out in pretty much the same way and gave it to Elektra to put on the compilation.

I was never a huge fan of doing cover songs. There's some great cover songs out there, and if a band wants to do one, I don't necessarily have a problem with it. I just always preferred to do something original if possible. So when we did end up doing a cover version, it was usually because of circumstance rather than choice.

Elektra didn't really mind, because 'Step On' was an Elektra song and ended up being a hit single instead of just being on a compilation that only came out in America, and they owned the publishing rights and everything. Plus they also got 'Tokoloshe Man' for the album, so it was a win–win for them. I liked our version of 'Tokoloshe Man'. It was a good tune, but I didn't want to release that ourselves as well because I was a bit paranoid about us being known for cover versions. Otherwise we might as well have just got in people like Nicky Chinn and Mike Chapman from Rak Records, who wrote all the hits for Mud. Most people still don't actually know that 'Step On' is a cover version and think we wrote it, because we brought a lot of different elements to it and made it our own. I actually got a message from John Kongos once, saying, 'Thanks for making my song so famous.'

When we reformed the Mondays in 1999, Simon Moran from SJM Concerts, who put the reunion together, wanted us to put out a new single to make a noise about us being back, but we weren't in the right frame of mind. At that stage, we were just doing it for the cash. But Simon had got us a deal with London Records to release a single and a new 'greatest hits' album, so we had to come up with something. In the end we decided to get Oakey and Osborne back again and do a cover of the classic Thin Lizzy single 'The Boys Are Back in Town', as it seemed apt. It also has a lot of Mancunian connections, which I'm not sure too many people know about. Phil Lynott was the lead singer of Thin Lizzy and his mum Phyllis used to have a legendary late-night drinking gaff in Whalley Range in Manchester called Phyllis's. It was a bit before my time. Its heyday was in the mid-seventies, when everyone from George Best to the Quality Street Gang used to drink in there. We weren't functioning great as a band then, and I thought our cover of 'The Boys Are Back in Town' was pretty terrible. I couldn't fucking believe it when we got a *Top of the Pops* appearance out of it, so I suppose it served its purpose and let people know the Mondays were back together and going out on tour. The tour sold out, anyway.

Just after the Mondays had got back together, I was approached by Salford opera singer Russell Watson to do a cover version of the Freddie Mercury and Montserrat Caballé song 'Barcelona' with him. Russell has gone on to sell millions of records and loads of platinum-selling albums, but he was still up-and-coming at the time and was just finishing his debut album, *The Voice*. We'd been playing 'Barcelona' before some of our reunion gigs, because Manchester United had got to the Champions League Final in Barcelona, and Russell had actually performed at the final, before the game. His manager, Perry Hughes, was also from Salford and I think he thought it might help broaden his appeal, make him look cool and help break him into a different market if he did a song with me. Russell had already recorded 'Barcelona' for his album before Perry came up with the idea of me guesting on it. When they suggested it to me, it was a bit of a no-brainer and I was like, 'Yeah, rightio. Bring it on.' I just popped into the studio and laid down my vocals on the track that was already laid down, then we went to Barcelona to do the video. Russell included the cover version on his album, and it went to No.1 in the classical charts in the UK and the US, and it was the first time a British artist had done that, so fair play to them. I certainly didn't expect to be singing on an album that was at No.1 in the classical charts on both sides of the Atlantic.

# Artwork

The artwork for singles and albums was always a huge deal for Factory Records – more than it was for most bands, to be honest. Tony Wilson always wanted every release to be important and look like a piece of art. A book celebrating Factory's artwork came out just before Wilson died in 2007, and he wrote the foreword and said: 'Why was packaging important to us? Because the job was a sacred one. Music had transformed our young lives, children of the sixties all. And now we were in the privileged position of putting out records ourselves. Does the Catholic Church pour its wine into mouldy earthenware pots? I think not.'

Typical Wilson. You could always rely on him to big up the significance of everything Factory did. But he was right: the covers and artwork at Factory had always been really important. I mean, the first album Factory ever released was *Unknown Pleasures*, which has what must be one of the most famous album covers of all time! The cover is more famous than the music, probably. I bet loads of kids who wear that *Unknown Pleasures* T-shirt haven't even got the album!

The cover of *Unknown Pleasures* was designed by Peter Saville, who was Factory's in-house designer and one of their founders, and he'd always done Joy Division and New Order's covers. But Saville didn't do the other bands on the label; they were done by other designers like Mark Farrow and Trevor Johnson, and right from the start Central Station did ours.

Central Station was started by two of my cousins, Matt and Pat. Pat was always into drawing and went and did art at Salford Tech, then got a job down in London designing record sleeves. Matt was working down in London as well, but then when everything started kicking off in Manchester with the Haçienda, they moved back and set up their own design studio. They used to go and see bands like the Ramones at the Free Trade Hall and they always liked the look of the old knackered train station next door, which was called Central Station. It had closed down at the end of the sixties, but they loved it so much they called their new design company after it. Central Station Design was Matt and Pat and Pat's girlfriend, Karen. It was just natural for Matt and Pat to do the artwork for us when we started putting records out. I can't remember having a sit-down and a discussion with Factory about it. I think it was just obvious to everyone they should do it, as they knew the band and where we were coming from better than anyone. They were there at the early gigs and even rehearsals, and Matt had even been in the first band I messed around with, before we got the Mondays together.

A bit like New Order and Saville, we just let Matt and Pat

get on with it. I don't think we ever had a meeting about the artwork, they just went off and did it. It was pretty different and more colourful and pop art than Saville's covers. Like I said, Saville had done Joy Division and New Order's covers, but other designers had done other bands on Factory, so it wasn't like we were snubbing Saville or anything.

Central Station had the idea of printing the name of the album on a separate see-through plastic sleeve, which cost quite a bit, and any normal record label would have said no, that's too expensive for a band's debut album but, Factory being Factory, they loved the idea and said yes. We were never really into having a picture of the band on the cover, we were always into having something more abstract. I think the only cover we're on is the early single 'Freaky Dancin'', which has individual small black-and-white pictures of us in the studio on the back.

For our second album, Central Station did this psychedelic painting of my face, which I wasn't sure about at first but everyone else loved it, and Factory ended up flyposting the outside of their offices with it. The inside sleeve was a vintage nude picture of a naked woman that Matt and Pat produced. We were living in Fallowfield, in a crazy house split into different flats. Matt and Pat used to score weed off this old couple called Ken and Maureen, who were naturists. They'd go round their house to score and they'd be sat there, watching *Coronation Street* starkers! They had a load of mad old polaroids they'd taken of each other in the seventies, which looked like stills from *Performance* – they had that kind of kinky, vintage vibe. Because we were obsessed by *Performance* at the time, and there's quotes from the film on the album, and the song 'Mad Cyril' is named after a character from the film, Matt and Pat decided to use this old naked polaroid of Maureen on the inner sleeve. Apparently, they were going to use a naked picture of Ken on the other side of the inner sleeve but they couldn't find any he was happy with. It got banned in some places. Tony Wilson called it 'one of the most profoundly disturbing inner sleeves in record history'.

For the cover of *Pills 'n' Thrills*, Matt and Pat came up with the idea of a montage of junk food and sweet wrappers from the States and back home. Apparently, Central Station wanted to reflect the fact that the album was recorded in Los Angeles and mixed in London. They were always like magpies, into collecting stuff like that. They even somehow persuaded Factory to pay for them to fly out to Los Angeles for a week to collect material to use! A week in LA, all expenses paid, just to pick up some fucking hot dog and sweet wrappers! That would never happen nowadays, and probably wouldn't have happened back then at any other record label. But Factory were just like, 'Yeah, if that's the concept, fine!' The irony is that when the album came out in the States, the label was worried they'd get done for copyright infringement by the sweet manufacturers, so they changed it anyway to some made-up sweet designs. Yet another brilliant Factory business decision!

Another of Matt and Pat's mad ideas was the melted plastic toys and letters on the cover of 'Judge Fudge'. You know those coloured plastic letters that stick on fridges that kids use to learn to spell? They spelled out the band name and the title of the single with those letters over a bunch of plastic toys, and then stuck them in the oven, but they couldn't get the door shut and nearly poisoned themselves with the fumes!

When we started Black Grape we still used Central Station. I remember when they used Carlos the Jackal on the front cover and there was a bit of aggro with the Americans, because they thought we were trying to glorify terrorism, but the band didn't even choose that. Matt and Pat just chose it because it was a really strong image. I never really used to pay that much attention to our artwork at the time, but – fair play to Central Station – when you look back at all the artwork they did, it's really strong. I've even got a few bits framed in my house now.

Artwork is less important now. It became less important when everyone was buying CDs rather than vinyl in the nineties, as obviously it's a much smaller space to work with so there's less you can do with it and people put less effort in. Most record companies were probably happy with that. Not many record companies thought like Factory and saw each release as a work of art. Then, when most people switched from CDs to streaming, even less effort was put in. I think most record companies thought there wasn't much point if all anyone is going to look at is a tiny thumbnail picture on their phone, which is a shame.

# Managers

In the nearly forty years I've been in the game, I've had every sort of manager going. From the useless to the big-time. From dealing with my dad to dealing with the mafia. I even managed the Mondays for a bit after we reformed, with Gaz Whelan, our drummer. I wouldn't recommend that. Don't ever manage yourself. Not only is it a load of hassle, it's also too close to home. It doesn't look great to the industry if you're handling all your affairs yourself, you need to get someone else to do it, you just need to find the right person for the stage you're at in your career.

When we first started, my dad managed us. He'd been a bit of a musician in his spare time when we were kids, playing the pubs and clubs around Salford. He once entered a talent competition and came second to Lisa Stansfield. By the time we started the band, he'd stopped doing his gigs, so he just transferred his energy to us. He did everything – drove the van, set the equipment up, tuned the guitars.

He even 'acquired' some of our equipment, 'accidentally' making off with the amplifiers or part of the PA from some working men's club. Even after he stopped managing us, he still did the sound on stage, mixing the monitors. When we played Wembley Arena for the first time, I couldn't hear myself properly and was mouthing to him 'I can't fucking hear it!' and he lost his rag and walked on stage and punched me in the face. In the middle of the fucking gig. That's not what you need, your dad walking on stage at Wembley and punching you in the face.

I knew my dad could only get us to a certain level, then we needed someone who could take us to the next level. That's when we met Phil Saxe, who ran a stall on the underground market in Manchester where we bought our flares. I got chatting to Phil and found out he was mates with Alan Erasmus and Mike Pickering at Factory Records, so I knew I had to get him to manage us, so we could get closer to Factory Records, and it worked. He put us under the noses of Factory, got us on the bill at a Battle of the Bands at the Haçienda and, before you know it, we were signed to Factory. Phil was a lovely guy and he was great for us at the time but, by the time we were coming to record our second album, I knew he had taken us as far as we could go, so I was starting to think about bringing someone else in to replace him.

I knew Nathan McGough through the Haçienda and Factory, and he was a huge fan of the Mondays and had been bending my ear about managing us. He was younger than Phil and had a bit more ambition about him, although a lot of that could have just been an age thing. Nathan was just a kid, really, as he was in his twenties, but he really understood where I wanted to go with the band at that stage, incorporating the acid house and Balearic influences and bringing in people like Paul Oakenfold to remix the band, and he worked brilliant for us, taking us to another level. He might have been young, but Brian Epstein was only a few years older than The Beatles, and Andrew Loog Oldham was actually younger than the Stones when he managed them.

I do remember just after Nathan started managing us, he got us our first £1000 gig, which was a bit of a big deal at the time, back in 1988. But Nathan took a girl back to the hotel with him after the gig, and when he woke up in the morning she was long gone and so was our £1000. So, Bez, our kid and PD all put bars of soap in pillowcases, threw Nathan in the hotel bath and beat him up with them. He was covered in bruises. That was Nathan's initiation to the band. That was us saying, 'Listen mate, we don't mind you partying as hard as us, but not if it's going to cost us money.'

The problem with Nathan was he was on it as much as us. Actually, that wasn't a problem. The problem was if he got a bit carried away… We didn't mind if he was as rock'n'roll as us if he didn't fuck up. If you've got me and Bez in the band you don't need the manager to be a loose cannon as well. It's great if you have a good relationship with your manager, but he can't be more rock'n'roll than you. I think that's a good rule for any band, but especially if you're Happy Mondays or Black Grape. Although, you know, it's a bit rich for me to tell someone they need to rein it in a bit and stop partying too hard. Especially back then, do you know what I mean?

After the Mondays split and I started Black Grape, I signed with a US management team, Gloria and Nik Nicholl, which was without doubt the worst decision I ever made. They were recommended by my American label, and they were an absolute disaster. They were always bigging up the fact that Gloria was the niece of Henry Hill from *Goodfellas*, as if that was supposed to impress me or scare me. As if. Do me a favour. Let's remember Henry Hill was basically a grass. The Nicholls saying they were related to him didn't intimidate me at all. After I fell out with the Nicholls I'd heard they'd said they were going to send some gangster over from New York to see me, and I just laughed. Stick someone on a plane to come and find me in Manchester if you want, but I can guarantee they won't be getting back on a plane to New York. Unsurprisingly, no gangster turned up. My short time with the Nicholls did cast a long shadow, though. They ended up suing me and, thanks to them, I couldn't earn any money for fourteen years. Any penny that I earned would be taken off me by the receivers. It took me a long time to resolve that.

After I sacked off the Nicholls, I knew I had to find a new manager and spoke to a few different people. I wasn't in great shape at the time. I had a meeting with Danny Goldberg, who was Nirvana's old manager, and he told me all about how he'd lost Kurt Cobain to heroin and asked me if I was on drugs. I obviously said no, but he could probably see in my eyes that I hadn't been to bed for days. So that didn't work out. I then met Richard Bishop, who managed Henry Rollins, and we got on. He ended up managing me for the second Black Grape album, although we had quite a distant relationship and in the end we both felt it wasn't really working, so we tore up the contract by mutual consent.

I'm now managed by Alan McGee, who's the best

manager I've ever had, and hopefully will be the last one I ever have. I want to stick to with Alan as long as I'm in the game. I've known Alan since the late eighties and he's been in the game for as long as I have, if not longer. He's from Glasgow and grew up with Bobby Gillespie and Primal Scream, started Creation Records and was the man who signed Oasis. When we met in the late eighties, he was living in Brighton, and Creation was based in London, but he was partying in Manchester all the time. He loved partying in Manchester and the Haçienda that much back in the day that he even got a flat in town for about six months, when acid house kicked off. He used to hang around Factory and the Haçienda quite a bit and was pally with Tony Wilson, as they were both running independent record labels. There was also the connection through Jeff Barrett, who worked closely with Alan at Creation in the early days and was then doing press for Factory and the Mondays, before he went on to set up Heavenly Records. Anyway, Tony arranged for Alan McGee to rent Alan Erasmus's flat. McGee was mates with Debbie Turner, who was in a band called Sister Lovers, and it was through her that he actually ended up signing Oasis. He went to see Sister Lovers in Glasgow, and Oasis had bullied themselves onto the bill. Alan saw them and signed them.

Alan said in his autobiography, 'I loved the Happy Mondays. I loved ecstasy. Happy Mondays had loads of ecstasy. It was a great arrangement.' My memory of those days is a bit hazier than Alan's but he remembers the night out he had in Manchester when he first understood acid house:

I made the mistake of asking Shaun Ryder for another one. He only gave me half a pill but it was the strongest pill I ever took. I was overheating, I had to lie on the floor. When I got up I was walking through the basement, looking at the beams in the ceiling, green diamonds and blue tessellating shapes. It was beautiful. Tony Wilson was there, in a shining white suit, like God, or a king. I found Debbie dancing and suddenly I was dancing too and I understood what the music was about. It was something new, something incredible. It felt like it was going to change everything.

At least I hadn't sold him a dud!

Shortly after that, Wilson invited Alan onto his *Granada News* show to talk about the music scene and asked him why he had moved to Manchester. 'A better class of drugs, Tony.' Even Tony wasn't expecting that response, live on the tea-time news. I bet some people choked on their tea, watching that.

Alan then persuaded Bobby Gillespie of Primal Scream to come up to Manchester and experience this amazing new scene. That's what acid house was like. It was like the worst secret in the world. Everyone would have their own epiphany and then would want to tell all their mates about it and get them to see the light. Anyway, that night, Alan remembers, 'I bought three Es off Shaun that night. They were twenty quid a go then. I bought two for me and one for Bobby. He was new to it: that would be more than enough for him, so I thought. I forgot, though, how dysfunctional Bobby's system is. The first one didn't touch the sides. He never came up at all. I was high as a kite. I had to give him my other one, much to my disappointment.' Gillespie and the Scream then got bang into acid house and started going to clubs like Shoom in London and Escape in Brighton. Although Bobby was never a dancer, as Alan says, 'While we were dancing Bobby Gillespie would be sitting on a wall, legs dangling like a Ramone, off his face on E.'

Jeff Barrett introduced them to Andrew Weatherall, and he ended up producing 'Loaded', which was his reworking of their single 'I'm Losing More Than I'll Ever Have', and then their breakthrough album *Screamadelica*, but you could say that all started when Alan and Bobby first came to the Haçienda and saw what was happening there and bought Es off me!

So, anyway, that's how far me and Alan go back. Like me, Alan's lived the life – or several lives – and has been through rehab and everything and is now clean, so we're on the same page there. We're men of a certain age who have seen the lot, and he just knows where I'm coming from, which makes life a lot easier. He's got a good idea of what I will and won't want to do, and I trust him to take care of everything.

# Awards

Some musicians love award ceremonies, but I've always been a bit hot and cold with them. Depends where my head was at that week, and which award ceremony it was. In the early days, I used to enjoy them as it was usually a free bar and it would be a good day out and you could catch up with a lot of people in other bands you hadn't seen for ages. But there is usually a lot of hanging around involved, which can get on your tits. They drag on for hours, some of these things. I'm also not the type who loves that sort of attention and getting my arse kissed. Some musicians lap that up, and they're the type who love an award ceremony, but it's never been my style. It depends which awards they are as well. It's a cliché to say it, but it does mean more if it's voted for by the fans or by fellow musicians. When it's just an award that is decided by a magazine, you can sometimes feel like they're ticking a box, that they want to make sure their awards look diverse, or sometimes it's pretty obvious they've almost invented an award for some rock star, just so they can invite them to the ceremony and get some press out of it. 'Look, we can give you this award, if you promise you'll turn up to accept it.' I think everyone in the industry knows a bit of that goes on.

One of the first ones we went to was the *Smash Hits* awards in 1990. Looking back, maybe we were a bit risqué to be invited to the *Smash Hits* awards, but we were more than happy to go because we just wanted to get the Mondays out there to as many people as possible. My main memory of those awards was that Jonathan King, the producer and presenter, was all over all the teeny boy bands, hanging around them like a bad smell, but he never came anywhere near us, he stayed well clear. Seemed a bit dodgy at the time to me, so it didn't surprise me at all later when he was banged up.

Then that same year, at the Q Awards we were up for album of the year for *Pills 'n' Thrills and Bellyaches*, and Oakey and Osborne were up for producer of the year for *Pills 'n' Thrills* as well. Paul McCartney was there, and Bill Wyman. That was when Paul McCartney said the Mondays reminded him of The Beatles in their *Magical Mystery Tour* phase, which we were all buzzing off.

When Oasis were coming through, Noel and Liam were always being bolshy and saying outrageous stuff and slagging everyone off at award ceremonies, and people lapped it up, but that was never my style. They were always picking a fight with someone. I remember when Noel slagged off Michael Hutchence at the Brit Awards and I felt really sorry for him. He was presenting an award to Oasis, and Noel got up and said,

'Has-beens shouldn't be presenting awards to gonna-bes.' I mean, I totally get where Noel was coming from – they were the hottest new band at the time and they were smashing it, and that cockiness was always part of their attraction. They'd slag off anyone and were usually pretty funny. But I don't think Noel had even met Hutchence then, and I had, and he was a dude. I'd spent some time with him when I was in Los Angeles and he was an absolutely top geezer with me. We used to have a few nights out in LA when I was over there, me and him hanging out in The Viper Room or wherever, and he really was a dude. So I didn't think Hutchence deserved that from Noel, as he was a pretty decent guy. I'm not sure how Noel feels about it now, after what happened to Michael. I've never asked him. But the way Noel was back then, he probably would have said something similar to whoever was presenting him with an award.

Probably the most memorable award ceremony for me was in 2000 when I was given an NME award for 'Godlike Services To Music'. Not memorable because I got the award, but for what happened afterwards. I got a bit bored at the awards, and I knew a heroin dealer who had a gaff nearby, so I nipped out of the ceremony to get some gear. I got to the gaff and spotted there were some police hanging around and it was a bit on top but I thought, 'Fuck it, I need my gear!' So I went in and, just as I'd bought the gear, the police came piling through the door and raided the place. Fortunately for me, one of the coppers recognized me, so I just said to him, under my breath, 'I'm just about to go and pick up an award, I'm up for Godlike Services to Music…' He looked at me, paused, shook his head and went, 'Go on, fuck off.' So that was a lucky escape. It didn't end there, though. I got back to the awards, or maybe it was the after-show party by that time, but anyway I got back there and at some stage in the proceedings I lost my mobile phone *and* my Godlike award. I did a phone-in with Chris Evans on his breakfast show in the morning, where I was supposed to be talking about the awards ceremony, but we just ended up talking about what had happened to me.

I lost half my awards over the years. Well, not lost. Our kid nicked half of them and sold them. There was a time when I didn't really have anywhere to live, and I had a load of them stashed at my mam's. When I went to get them back later, he'd had them away and flogged them. I managed to get a couple replaced, but the rest of them were gone.

It's nice to get some recognition but, out of all the awards I've won, I did really appreciate winning The Ivors Inspiration Award at the Ivor Novello Awards in 2016. That was a good one to get because you're getting real recognition. It feels like a proper award. It's one of the only awards that isn't influenced by record companies and is actually decided by your peers and other songwriters, so I appreciated that. It was a good day out as well, very sedate compared to back in the day.

# Fans

When we first made it, camera phones were still a thing of the future, so if I got stopped by a fan it was usually just for an autograph, and maybe someone would want a bit of a chat. When camera phones came in that obviously changed things, and everyone wants a picture now, don't they? I don't mind doing one, but you just need to be careful if you do one in a busy public place. Quite a few people might have clocked you, and not said anything, but as soon as one person asks for a selfie then all of a sudden everyone else wants one.

I've never had a stalker, but I did have someone passing themselves off as me once. After the Mondays split, some stories started going round about me signing on the dole in Salford. Piers Morgan still had my number from when he went to Brazil with us, and he rang me one morning and said, 'Look, Shaun, someone's given us some photos of you signing on.' I was like, 'What?! Piers, you know me, mate.

If you've got photos, *look* at them, because I'm telling you, it's *not* me, mate.' So Piers said, 'Do you need money?' and I said, 'Piers, look, between you and me, I'm already putting a new band together. Why would I be signing on the dole, Piers, you know what I mean? Check your source and check your photographs.' Anyway, less than two hours later, Piers calls me back and agrees it isn't me in the photos and it's a load of bollocks. But apparently there was some kid in the dole office in Salford posing as Shaun Ryder, signing on and claiming for whatever he could claim for.

Of all the places we went in the world, Japan and Brazil were pretty wild for the reaction we got from fans. Everyone knows the Japanese go crazy for British bands, and it was pretty fucking mad. I was followed down the street and so were Bez and Gaz Whelan. You'd just nip out for a little walk from the hotel, and you'd have like a hundred young Japanese girls following you. They'd ask you for your autograph and you'd give them one, but they'd still keep following you.

When we first arrived in Brazil, back in 1991, they whisked us straight off the plane and we thought we were being nicked at first, but they just escorted us through to this private courtyard car-park bit, which wasn't open to the public. It was a back entrance that I think was used for police and immigration staff or something, but – even there, which wasn't open to the public – there were hundreds of fans, almost all female. Someone who worked at the airport must have let them in, and they were all trying to get onto the bus and screaming, 'Take us with you, please!' and stuff like that. There were mothers in their thirties and forties, holding their teenage daughters up and saying, 'Take my daughter with you!' It was fucking crazy!

As I mentioned in the Fame chapter, I get recognized everywhere, it's just how you handle it. I tend to avoid pubs and clubs when I'm at home and just chill with my family now, but if I am out working in Manchester or London, I might nip in a pub for a drink, and then I'll nearly always get someone coming over. The thing is, people still think Shaun Ryder is always looking for a fucking party. I'm nearly sixty and people still think I want to get on it all the time. You generally get two types – you get people my age, in their fifties, who are still throwing pints down their neck like they're twenty-three and want to get pissed. They start chatting to you and, before you know it, you've got eighteen pints in front of you, and five or six whisky chasers. Then you've got the young-uns, who want to get on it, and keep offering me a line, like I'm going to want to do a line in the afternoon. Because my reputation precedes me, everyone wants to tell their mates they've had a pint or a line with Shaun Ryder.

# Festivals

I never went to festivals before I was in a band. They weren't such a big deal when I was a kid. There was only a handful of festivals back then. It's only the last twenty years that the festival scene has exploded. Now it seems like there's a dozen different big festivals every weekend, and bands can spend most of their summer bouncing around the country, playing different festivals. You can even play two or three in a weekend sometimes.

The first big festival we ever did was Glastonbury, when we headlined it. Talk about in at the deep end. We'd played a couple of small-ish festivals, like a thing at Belle Vue in Manchester and some little festival in Finsbury Park in London, but they were to only a few hundred people. We jumped from there to headlining the Pyramid Stage at Glastonbury.

It was quite an eventful weekend. We went down on our tour bus, and had a big entourage with us. Our driver crashed the bus into a tree as we arrived on site, and put the windscreen through, so that was a good start. Some of our lot made copies of our backstage passes and were then selling them outside and made a right few quid. I think they even had a colour photocopier and a laminating machine on the bus.

We were also selling bootleg T-shirts, as well as our official merchandise on the official stalls. You can never stop people selling bootleg T-shirts, so we decided we might as well bootleg ourselves and clean up. One of our lads who was bootlegging, John the Phone, was actually kidnapped that weekend at Glastonbury. Some fucking biker crew grabbed him and took him to some disused farmhouse, tied him up, shaved his head and beat him up to try and find out where he'd stashed all the money he made. But, fair play to John the Phone, he never told them and eventually he was let go.

I wasn't interested in the hippy, mystical side of Glastonbury, that's just not my thing. Glastonbury in 1990 was still quite basic. It wasn't much different to how it had been in the seventies. Nothing like it is now, with models and half of West London floating about, looking like they're in a fashion shoot. In 1990 it was still pretty rough. I was addicted to heroin at that time, and I can't really remember much of the performance at all, I'm afraid. Bez used to go every year to Glastonbury, but it's not really my scene. I'm not one for camping. Bez always seemed to get into mither there as well. He actually got arrested there for drug dealing one year, put in a police van and carted off. There was another year when he lost his false teeth, and some girl found him in a hedge at 5 a.m. looking for his teeth. I remember him and Mani had a DJ gig at Turnmills in London on the Saturday night of Glastonbury once. They'd been at Glastonbury since the Thursday or something, mindless, up for days with no sleep, then got someone to drive them back to London to DJ for a couple of hours on the Saturday night, then drove straight back down to Glastonbury after that – 24-hour party people, no days off.

The biggest ever festival we did was Rock in Rio, in Brazil, in 1991. When we first got offered the festival we just thought, 'Brazil? Top! We're up for that!' We'd never been to South America at the time, so we were buzzing. We didn't realize quite how big a gig it was going to be. There were 198,000 people there. That's three times the size of Glastonbury at the time. It was also broadcast to 60 million people, so it was huge. It was a nine-day event at the Maracanã stadium, Brazil's national stadium, and we were playing on the eighth night, with A-ha and a few other bands.

When we landed in Brazil, the first thing we saw was a huge story about the Mondays in the papers with a big headline saying, 'ECSTASY DEALERS COME TO RIO!' I'd done a telephone interview with the Brazilian music press before we came and was just joking with the journalist. He said, 'So, you will bring ecstasy with you to Brazil, yes?' and I said, 'Yeah, course mate, I'm going to bring fucking tons of it with me! Do you want some? I'll bring you some over!' But this dude had done a number on us and given my quotes to the Brazilian tabloids, who'd made it into a huge story.

We got into a few scrapes on that trip. One day I needed to score, so me and our tour manager took a taxi up into one of the favelas to this dealer's gaff. I got my gear and did it there and then, but it was pretty strong, so I went into this real nodding state and needed to get my head down. The problem was this dealer's gaff was just one room with no bed. His grandma had just died, though, and they already had the coffin there waiting for her. I needed to get my head down so badly that I just dived in his grandma's coffin and got my head down for half an hour. The dealer was fine with it.

When it came to the actual festival performance, our set didn't start well. You don't get a chance to do a proper soundcheck at festivals and we had a few technical issues at the start. Then the heavens opened and there was a thunderstorm during our set. My dad was still one of our roadies at the time, and he had written all my lyrics out for me on big sheets with marker pen so I could remember them, and they were taped to the stage, but the rain smudged them all and made the ink run so I couldn't read anything. So I just had to ad-lib through a lot of the set, which took us back to how we used to be in the rehearsal room in the Boardwalk. It was great, and some people who were there have said it was our greatest ever set.

At the height of the Manchester scene, someone decided they'd put a festival on in Heaton Park in North Manchester. It was rarely used for gigs back then and the last big crowd there had been for Pope John Paul II in 1982. Oasis later played there, in 2009, and Liam told the crowd: 'Last time I was here I came to see the Pope. He was all right but he didn't have many tunes.' Now it's used every summer for Parklife festival, which has over 80,000 kids going mental. Back in 1991, there was a two-day festival called Cities in the Park, featuring almost every band on Factory, plus Bernard

Sumner and Johnny Marr's Electronic and a few random others like De La Soul and The Wonder Stuff. We headlined the last night, and just after I arrived a load of lads from Salford rushed the gate and a few hundred people got in for free. The backstage area was full of blaggers that day. Mental. Alan Wise, who used to put New Order gigs on, was the promoter, and at one point he said he might as well turn the stage round because there were more blaggers backstage than there were actual audience members out front.

I had another incident with remembering my lyrics when we played Coachella Festival in Palm Springs, after we finished the *Uncle Dysfunktional* album. Elliot Rashman was managing us at the time. It was not long before Tony Wilson died, and Elliot had arranged for Wilson, who was quite ill at that stage, to introduce us and he gave a typically Wilsonesque speech about the Mondays pulling together 'the house music of Chicago and Detroit with punk rock' and how 'they changed the world'. Very Tony. Unfortunately, some idiot in management had decided that – for the sake of saving some fucking poxy amount like £200 – we would hire an autocue in America rather than take one with us, and it was the wrong format. I can't remember the exact technical details, but I know it wasn't compatible and I was left with no fucking autocue. So, after Tony's intro bigging us up, I ended up just trying to bumble my way through some of the songs. All so that we could save £200.

These days I'll do a bunch of festivals each summer. Some with the Mondays and some with Black Grape. Depending on what festival it is, we can draw a pretty wide-ranging audience. You get all the fifty-year-olds who remember the

Mondays from the first time round, but now we also get their kids and a younger audience. Either their parents have got them into us or they've seen me and Bez on *Gogglebox* or something and then gone and checked out our music and decided we're all right.

Festivals are also a lot better organized than they were back in the day, and obviously we don't have the chaos and huge entourage surrounding us that the Mondays used to have, which makes things easier. We don't have people flogging our backstage passes or anything any more!

# Touring the world

I've been lucky enough to go round the world loads of times as a musician. I say 'lucky', but it's not always as glamorous as people think it is. No one really wants to hear a rock star moaning about how hard their life is, so I'll spare you that, but Charlie Watts pretty much nailed it. On the Rolling Stones' twenty-fifth anniversary, Charlie was asked how he felt about it, and he said those twenty-five years had basically been five years' work and twenty years' hanging around. I know how he feels. A lot of touring is just endless hanging around. That's partly why so many bands party so much and drink so much when they're on tour – to take away the monotony of all the hanging around.

When we first started touring other countries back in the day, you did wonder if they were going to get the Mondays, to get where we're coming from. It gets easier once you've reached a certain level in that country and they know a bit about you and what to expect. One thing the Americans could never get their head around was Bez. The British loved Bez. They always have. He's like a folk hero to the British people. Here in Britain, Bez almost *was* the Happy Mondays at one point, or at least he personified us. Sometimes he would get the biggest cheer of the night when he came on stage. People would be cheering him on, shouting, 'Go on, Bez!' If people love a band and dream about being in that band, they usually want to be the front man or the guitarist, but with us a lot of people wanted to be Bez. They could see themselves in Bez. It was a different case over in America. The Yanks always struggled to get their head around the idea of Bez. They never really grasped the concept of Bez. They would be like, 'What does that guy *do*, man? He's not a dancer – that's not dancing.' Well, he's not really a dancer, no. 'So, what does he *do*? He doesn't *sing*, he doesn't play *anything*. He just fucks about on stage off his head.' The British loved the fact that Bez didn't really do anything – they celebrated that – but the Yanks just couldn't understand it. As far as a lot of them are concerned, they've paid to come and see a band and on stage they want to see a band, with everybody doing a specific job, so they couldn't see what Bez was doing there, this guy with bulging eyes, wandering up and down the stage.

I wouldn't say geography is my strong point, but if you think I'm bad, you should see Bez. I remember one of the first times we went to the States on tour, and we were doing a press conference one day. The journalist would stand up and say their name and what paper they worked for before asking their question. This one journalist stood up and said their name, and said, '*Daily News*, Pennsylvania,' and Bez went 'Mega! Where Dracula is from?'

His unusual grasp of geography was also highlighted in an interview when we were recording *Pills 'n' Thrills* in Los Angeles. Terry Christian from *The Word* came over to film an interview with us. *The Word* was a pretty big deal at the time, as everyone watched it on Friday night when they got in from the pub, but I couldn't really be arsed with it. He interviewed us on the beach at Santa Monica, and asked: 'You're supposed to be going on tour to Japan next. What have you heard about Japan?'

'I've heard, it's mega,' said Bez, 'full of fucking... Chinese.'

We did get quite a lot of hassle from customs back in the day, when we were passing through as a band. Sometimes because our reputation preceded us and sometimes just because we looked like a gang of ruffians. I've been strip-searched more times than I care to remember. Not that I want to remember even one of the times. They used to stick you on this glass toilet so they could make sure nothing was coming out. I even wrote a song about it on *Pills 'n' Thrills* called 'Holiday': 'Hold it there boy, is that your bag... /I'm here to harass you/I want your pills and grass you/You don't look first class you/Let me look at your arse you.' Nowadays, it makes a refreshing change to not have to worry myself when I get to the airport about whether there's anything in the bottom of my bag that I've forgotten about, or checking all my pockets and wondering if the sniffer dogs will be able to sniff any remnants of last night on me.

We've had a few problems getting into countries and getting refused entry as well, over the years. The first time it was a real problem was in 1995, when we were supposed to go on tour to the States with Black Grape. I'd got a ten-year passport in 1985, which was one of those old black ones. They didn't have an electronic chip in them, so your criminal record didn't automatically pop up on screen when you went through customs, so I just simply lied on all the immigration forms where they asked about convictions. But when I applied for a new passport, I got one of the new maroon EU ones that have a chip in them, and my criminal record now appeared on their screens. When we applied for visas to tour the States, I was refused one and so was Kermit. Part of the problem was my importation charge from years ago, when I was caught bringing a bit of weed back from Amsterdam. Importation is miles worse than possession in customs' eyes. It didn't matter that it was only a little bit of weed; to them, importation is importation, so I might as well have been Al Capone. They checked their records and realized I had been lying to them for ten years and I got an automatic ban from the States for a while.

Because we couldn't get into America, we decided to do a press trip for the Americans to Cuba. The idea was to invite all the American press to Cuba and we could do the interviews there. We were only in Cuba for a few days, and I can't remember too much about the trip because I wasn't too well. I did worry for a minute a few years later when a mate of mine asked me if I met Castro when we were in Cuba, and I couldn't remember. I had to check and thankfully I was assured I didn't. I don't mind only having a hazy memory of Cuba, but I would hate it if I'd met Castro and not remembered it!

We got into a lot of mad scrapes back in the day, but nowadays I'm pretty chilled if we're on tour somewhere.

As soon as the gig is over, I'll be back to the hotel. I don't usually bother with the after-show parties or any of that, as that tends to lead to trouble, and it's also where I'll get mithered the most. So I'll be straight back to the hotel, maybe have a couple of drinks in the hotel bar, but I'll be in bed by midnight, usually before the hotel bar even closes.

# The tour bus

I 've had every type of experience on a tour bus. As you can probably imagine, the Mondays and Black Grape tour buses were quite debauched back in the day. When we went on tour with New Order, and then Terry Hall and The Colourfield, my dad would hire a Transit from Salford Van Hire, and we threw these brown sofa cushions from Gaz's house in the back and a sleeping bag each. We'd all be in the back, fucking freezing. After we did a gig in Reading one night, we all had to sleep in the back of the van at a motorway services. It was February and when we woke up there was ice on the inside of the windows. We were all still on the dole, and as we started to do gigs further afield, someone would always miss their signing-on day, which meant you'd get no money. So in the end we started paying our mates a fiver to go and sign on for us.

One up from the Transit van would be a splitter van, which is split half between a minibus and a Transit. You have a few seats and table in the front, and then a van bit at the back to chuck all your instruments in. Then you get a decent minibus and when you're on tour, you've got a tour manager who takes care of everything for you. Once you reach a certain level, everything is done for you. You don't need to think about where you need to be or even when you need to eat or drink. The tour manager just gets you on the bus each day and then tells you what's happening that day.

There was a few scenes on the Mondays tour bus in the film *24 Hour Party People*, and that was pretty close to how it was in reality back then. It was pretty wild. Tim Burgess has talked about how The Charlatans got so bored on the tour bus, on long journeys, that they used to blow cocaine up each other's arses, which is something that Fleetwood Mac also used to do. I mean, there were a lot of drugs on the Mondays tour bus back in the day, but that's something I never did. Can you imagine me trying to blow coke up Bez's arse? No thanks. I'd rather eat a crocodile's penis in the jungle.

I remember at the end of Black Grape, when it was all going a bit tits up, our tour manager Muzzer used to sleep with the briefcase with the tour float and takings in it. He would have it in his bunk with him. Sometimes he even handcuffed himself to it. That's how bad the mood had got in the band and on the tour bus. There were too many drugs around and no one trusted each other. It was like the end of the Mondays again, a sinking ship. On the second-to-last night of the tour in Glasgow, there were huge arguments again on the bus, and I'd just had enough. Muzzer was asleep on the couch with the briefcase with all the cash in, and I just sneaked it off him and did one in the night. It was a bit like that scene in *Trainspotting* where Renton sneaks the money off Begbie after they've done their big drug deal. I think there was only about two grand in there, but I just had it away and did one, and that was the end of Black Grape. Although the writing had been on the wall anyway.

I used to actually live on the tour bus for a very short while, when the Mondays first got back together in 1999. The Mondays had sold out Manchester Arena, and it was our biggest ever hometown gig. We were the returning heroes – the boys were back in town – but in reality the truth was I was a bit on my arse, and I spent the night before the gig sleeping in the tour bus behind the stage in the Arena as I didn't really have anywhere else to crash.

We did once have a mentalist Scottish bus driver who, when he had a drink, would really go on the turn. Proper Jekyll and Hyde dude. We all went for an Indian meal in Stockport and he'd had a drink and had a row with the waiter. I can't remember what happened but he got chucked out – and probably deservedly so, as when he'd had a drink he could be a right liability. Anyway, unbeknown to us, after we'd paid up and left and all gone back to the hotel, he went back there with a baseball bat to try and have it out with the waiter as the restaurant was closing. First we knew about it was when the police turned up at the hotel and wanted to search us all and speak to us. Like I said earlier, the last thing we wanted back in the day was for anyone to be doing anything that would bring things on top and get the police involved, especially your bloody bus driver, so we had to get rid of the mentalist Scottish dude after that.

We don't have a big tour bus for all the band nowadays. I have my own personal road manager, Wayne, who drives me about everywhere. I don't travel with the rest of the band, and Bez doesn't either – he has his own driver or his missus will drive him. The rest of the band will all be on a splitter tour bus, and me and Bez will arrive separately. It's better that way, as it means we're not all in each other's pockets the whole time.

# Musical differences

I t's become such a cliché for bands to say they've split up because of musical differences. That used to make me laugh because most of the time it's bollocks. It's not musical differences, it's ego differences. They might dress it up as arguments about music direction, but really, behind that, it's people's noses getting out of joint. People thinking, 'Why is he getting all the attention? Why is everyone looking at him, not me?' Once you become successful, every person in the band gets to thinking that they are the real genius behind the band and forgets what made the band was the chemistry between the members.

Ian Brown said, 'You'll never find a Manchester band slagging off another Manchester band, but within each Manchester band, people will rip each other apart; Mondays, Smiths, New Order, Roses, Oasis. No one will slag each other off, but inside the band, they'll rip each other to death!' He's right. It happened with my band – both my bands! – and it happened with his band too. Then you get back together and bury the hatchet, then the same thing happens all over again.

It's even trickier when it's your brother in the band, like me and our Paul. If you think of any brothers in bands, they're always falling out and at war with each other. Just look at Noel and Liam Gallagher. The dynamic of Oasis was based on their tempestuous relationship, and the press and fans were fascinated by it, but in the end that's what broke the band up. I remember once when I wasn't getting on with our Paul, walking into some award ceremony with Joanne and he was there sat with Noel and Liam, and I said to Joanne, 'I'm not sitting with him. Come on, let's sit over here.' Liam came over, trying to smooth things over, saying, 'Come on, I know what it's like with brothers.'

Just look at any brothers in bands. Ray Davies and Dave Davies in The Kinks used to tear each other apart and didn't talk to each other for years. The Beach Boys, The Jackson 5, they all had their issues. Even Bros fucking hated each other for years, as that recent documentary showed. The Kemp brothers from Spandau Ballet, Gary and Martin, always seemed to get on, and they even went on to act together, but I think they're the exception to the rule.

You could argue that musical differences over *Yes Please!* played a part in the Mondays splitting up, as I certainly wasn't vibing off the music that the rest of the band came up with in the studio. But again, I think that was more down to ego than anything. Instead of playing what was right for the band, or right for the song, they all went off on their own trip, everyone wanting their parts to be up front in the mix. A similar thing happened with Kermit at the end of

Black Grape. He started believing what people were saying in his ear, that he should really be as big as Tupac, and I was holding him back, when in reality he'd only ever really achieved success with me in Black Grape.

Hopefully we're over all that now, in the Mondays and Black Grape, as everyone is a bit older and wiser, and I think we all appreciate what it was that made the Mondays and Black Grape great, rather than our egos demanding that we all need to prove ourselves individually all the time, which is exhausting and only ends up splitting a band up.

It wasn't me who split the Mondays up, but I think we all probably played some part in it. All I would advise is just don't start believing you're Charlie Big Potatoes and thinking you don't need the rest of the band. Just try and remember that it was the combination of different people in the band that made the music that got you where you are.

# Teeth

I was never really bothered about my teeth. I actually had really good teeth as a kid; they were perfect and white and everything. But by the time I was forty, my lifestyle had fucked them up. It was a combination of bad diet and some of the drugs I'd done, particularly smoking crack cocaine. It's the coke that fucks up your teeth rather than heroin. It wasn't a vain thing to get my teeth done. It wasn't like I wanted a perfect pair of Hollywood gnashers. They were done out of necessity more than anything. I knew I needed to get them sorted and then I just received the offer of a free set of teeth out of the blue one day.

After the Mondays made it, I used to spend a lot of money in the Armani shop in Manchester, and I met this kid called Lance who was working in there while he was training to be a dentist. Lance used to make a hell of a lot of money off me in commission, because I was spending so much in the shop. Years later, in 2005, he got back in touch and told me he now had his own practice in St Ann's Square. He offered to give me a whole new set of teeth, which cost a good £20,000 or £30,000, in exchange for a bit of publicity. The only downside was the whole world was going to see how bad my teeth were because Lance wanted to take some 'before and after' shots. *Granada Reports* also came down and did a little item on my teeth.

Normally, if you were having a complete new set, you would have it done in loads of one- or two-hour sessions, but I just had it done in two eight-hour stints. I hate going to dentists more than most people and have done since I was a kid; it's almost a phobia with me. I remember seeing the school dentist once, when I was ten, and the anaesthetic didn't take at first so I had to have a few injections and it freaked me out a bit. So after I left school, I didn't go to the dentist for a long time, which is probably why my teeth got into the state that they did. I only went when I got really bad toothache, and even then I'd just say to the dentist, 'Here's £50. Just pull this tooth out, will you?' Nobody in their right mind sits in the dentist's chair for eight hours, but Lance said he could do it in two eight-hour stints if I could handle it, so I agreed. I just wanted to get it over with. I only had a local anaesthetic, but it didn't hurt as much as I thought it might do. I thought I would need loads of Valium to get me through it, but Lance made me as comfortable as possible and it wasn't as bad as I thought. The smell was actually the worst thing about it. When they were sawing and grinding down my old teeth, there was this horrible smell of burning bone.

# Reality TV

I 'll admit I couldn't really see the attraction of reality TV when it first took off. I used to get badgered to do loads of reality TV shows and always turned them down. Not necessarily because I thought it was uncool or I was above it or anything. I just didn't watch those kinds of shows at the time and hadn't quite realized how big they had become. But I changed my mind after I saw what happened to Bez with *Celebrity Big Brother*.

It's mad how much reality TV has taken off over the past few years. Back in the nineties, when we first became famous, there wasn't really any reality TV. Clive James had a late-night TV show back in the day, and he used to show clips of Japanese shows where they got contestants to do crazy stuff, and everyone would laugh at it and think, 'They're fucking mad, the Japanese!' Ten years later it was all over British TV, and they've got celebs in the jungle doing exactly the same sort of stunts we used to laugh at the Japanese for doing!

I was asked to do *Celebrity Big Brother* at the start of 2005, but I've never liked the programme, so I passed it on to Bez. I'd watched a bit of it before he was on, and didn't like the way they treated the housemates. They seemed to deliberately pick people who have slight mental issues, lock them together in a little house, then just chuck booze at them and stir things up to get a reaction. It seemed manipulative and a bit wrong to me at the time. I also still had legal issues with my ex-management going on at the time, and they were taking all my earnings, so there was no way I was going to do a big show like that if all the money was going straight to those idiots.

I watched a bit of it when Bez was on, but no way did I expect him to win. I don't think anyone did at first. But there's a lot of normal folk who watch those shows, and some of the celebs just come across as absolute dicks. You really see some of them for what they are – just pricks with big egos and small talent. So if you come across as someone who's pretty down to earth, then all of a sudden everyone warms to you a bit and is rooting for you.

What I totally didn't expect, and Bez didn't either, is what it would do for his profile and fame. When he came out of the house, he was the most famous man in Manchester. He wasn't the guy who a few people knew as that bloke who used to be the dancer in Happy Mondays, a bit of a fun figure. Now he was *Bez*, this new celebrity figure. Seriously. He was much more famous than he was before, and he was getting offers to do all sorts of stuff. It really brought home to me how these shows could raise your profile. At the end of the day, that's what you did *Top of the Pops* for back in the day, wasn't it? To raise your profile, get your music heard by more people and sell more records and more gig tickets. Reality shows are now just the modern way of raising your profile. *Top of the Pops* is gone, and they're now the most popular shows.

That said, I'm still not a fan of a lot of the reality shows on TV. They're very hit and miss. Some of them I quite like, but others I can't stand. Particularly something like *Love Island*, which is just bollocks. Utter bollocks. Just shallow dickheads squabbling over nothing. If I want to listen to children squabbling, I can just go and stand outside my kids' rooms, you know what I mean?

Once I came round to the idea of doing reality TV and could see the value of it, then I just wanted to make sure I did the right show. I don't mind making a bit of a fool of myself for entertainment, but I'm not going to put up with someone trying to make a fool of me, you know? I'm fine with pretty much anything if we're all in on the joke, but don't take the piss and try and make me the butt of a joke. When I signed up for *I'm A Celebrity… Get Me Out Of Here!*, I knew they were going to get me to eat a monkey's penis or whatever, but they do it to everyone, so you're all in the same boat. When I got asked to go on *Strictly Come Dancing*, I knew that would be different. I knew they wanted me on there as a bit of a joke because half the contestants are athletes or pop stars whose career has been based on dance routines, and then there would be Shaun Ryder trying to do the foxtrot or whatever as a bit of a joke. No thanks, mate.

There's probably some hardcore Mondays fans who think me and Bez shouldn't be doing reality TV, because it's not rock'n'roll or 'not very Mondays', but you're always going to get some idiots like that. They'd sooner see you struggling and on your arse a bit than doing something that's 'not rock'n'roll' in their eyes. But they're in the minority and, with all respect, bollocks to them. They don't get to decide what is rock'n'roll, and they don't get to tell me and Bez what Happy Mondays and Black Grape are about. You have to adapt to stay in this game, and I don't have a problem with that. Is 'Wrote For Luck' a worse song because I went in the jungle? Don't be daft. Are Happy Mondays less cool because Bez went in the *Big Brother* house? Don't be stupid. It just means more new people get to hear 'Wrote For Luck' than if I hadn't gone in the jungle or Bez hadn't gone on *Big Brother*. As a band you need to bring the younger generation as well, and that's where reality TV comes in. You have to be more of an all-round entertainer now, and doing the odd bit of reality TV is just part of that. You just need to be careful that you pick the right show. Look at someone like Alesha Dixon or Ricky Wilson, who have done well on big TV shows. They've come from a music background but now they have become more of an all-round entertainer.

I know I need to do that daytime TV stuff now, and I'm comfortable with it. Twenty years ago, the idea of me going on a show like *Loose Women*, chatting to a load of middle-aged women to an audience of housewives, would have been mental. Although the producers of *Loose Women* probably wouldn't have dreamed of inviting me on there twenty years ago, as they would have been too wary of me! But now I'm totally fine with it. I see the value and point of doing shows like that, and I don't mind them. In fact, I quite like them.

In recent years I've been offered lots of different weird reality and celebrity shows. It's a bit like that Alan Partridge sketch where he's coming up with random ideas for TV shows like 'Youth Hostelling with Chris Eubank' and 'Monkey Tennis'. In fact, 'Youth Hostelling with Chris Eubank' is about the only thing I haven't been offered. I might have been up for it if I had been offered it, though, as I used to know Eubank a bit from when we both lived in the Landmark Hotel at the same time. So, in a way, I've already done it!

One of the first of those types of shows I was offered was called *Celebrity Shark Bait*, and they said it would involve me and Richard E. Grant swimming with crocodiles and sharks. I thought they were joking at first. God knows who comes up with these ideas! Me and Richard E. Grant swimming with sharks?! I turned that down and I presumed he did too. But then I heard a bit later that he had actually said yes to it! They went ahead with it, and he ended up doing it with Ruby Wax and Colin Jackson.

We did do *Ghosthunting With Happy Mondays*, with Yvette Fielding, in 2009, just for a laugh. You know what you're signing up for with a show like that, and part of the deal is you're supposed to ham it up a bit. It would be even more ridiculous if you took it seriously, although I do think Bez was a bit freaked out. It reminded me of when I first met him twenty-five years earlier, and Bez would come round and we'd take acid and watch a vampire film or some Peter Cushing Hammer film, and Bez would get freaked out and wouldn't want to go home on his own. He'd have to stay the night because he was still tripping and didn't want to walk home in the dark, off his head.

If you're going to do these things, you've just got to roll with it. There's no point agreeing to do it and then being arsey. It's like when Peter Kay asked me and Bez to be in the video to 'Amarillo' – he just wanted me swigging a beer and Bez doing his dance behind him. I was fine with it. Peter Kay wasn't taking the piss out of me and Bez, because everyone in that video was laughing at themselves a little bit, from Ronnie Corbett to Rod Hull. You can't take yourself so seriously that you can't do something like that. Grannies were getting off on that 'Amarillo' video. Stuff like that makes you a household name.

When I got asked to go into the jungle to do *I'm A Celebrity...* in 2010, the timing just felt right. If they had asked me a couple of years earlier, I probably would have said no. But, like I say, I'd seen the benefit of doing reality TV shows after Bez won *Celebrity Big Brother*, and the record company were also keen for me to do it. Everything has changed over the years, and if you want to get your record into places like Sainsbury's, then you need to be on a prime-time television show. Joanne and my kids all watched *I'm A Celebrity...* at home, so they also helped persuade me to do it. Also, John Lydon, lead singer from the Sex Pistols, had done it a few years before, so I thought, 'If it's good enough for Johnny Rotten, it's good enough for me.' Ant and Dec were old Mondays and Black Grape fans from back in the day, so they were made up when I agreed to do the show.

They don't really prepare you much before you go into the jungle, as they want to get your reactions, and your shock and surprise, when things happen. I did have a couple of meetings with the producers, and Daisy Moore, who was in charge of celebrity shows at ITV back then, said to me, 'You're going to hate me when you come out of the jungle.' But I didn't. If anything, it wasn't as bad as I thought it was going to be.

A lot of the other more mainstream celebrities don't think it through and think they can go into the jungle and keep up the public façade of who they are. Not possible. Apart from the fact that they're not going to have their stylists and hair and make-up artists and their whole entourage, within a few hours of getting in there, you're tired and hungry. I don't care who you are or how bothered you are about your public image, when you're tired and hungry the true you comes out. But that didn't bother me. I knew going in there that people would see the real me. If anything, that was a bonus for me, because most people only knew the caricature of Shaun Ryder as a drug-taking maniac, when I knew that was only one side to the real me, and I was happy for people to see what I was really like.

Thankfully I didn't get stuck with too many luvvies or idiots in the jungle. I had seen a few bits of previous years, when Joanne and the kids had it on, and I remember seeing Paul Burrell, Princess Diana's former butler, behaving like a real knob. He was giving it, 'You'll never guess who rang me one night? Tom!' One of the others said, 'Tom who?' and he said, 'Tom Hanks!' I just thought, 'What a prick!'

I probably got on best with Nigel Havers when I was in there, and Dom Joly, who had been a Mondays fan and was telling me about watching us on *Top of the Pops* when he was at uni. Lembit Öpik was all right, and Jenny Eclair and

Stacey Solomon were great. It was only Gillian McKeith who was a bit of a dick. She just had no manners.

I wasn't arsed about any of the tasks like eating weird things. That didn't really bother me. The only two real problems I had were right at the start when I had to jump out of the helicopter, and then when that snake bit me. Jumping out of the helicopter didn't scare me, it was the fact that I was struggling to breathe through my nose. Nothing to do with drugs, although I have put enough of them up there in the past. No, it's actually a hereditary condition. A lot of our family had sinus problems, and my mam even had a bone taken out of her nose so she could breathe properly. Hanging out of a helicopter at 12,000 feet, it's almost impossible to breathe through your mouth, so I was really struggling. I thought I was going to pass out on live TV at one stage, like a right goon. I was pretty relieved when I got down on the ground. Then when the snake bit me, during one of the bushtucker trials, it really did hurt. It sank its teeth into my hand and the little fucker wouldn't let go. I gritted my teeth and went, 'You little…' but managed not to swear. I could see the snake handlers panicking, but my instinct just told me to keep calm. It actually took them about forty minutes to get the little shit off me, and the doctors gave me Valium to calm me down.

More recently, me and Bez got asked to do *Celebrity Gogglebox*. I knew it would be the right sort of show for us to do because it just shows us how we are – two middle-aged blokes who used to cane it, sat at home watching the box, having a laugh and comparing our different memories of how things were with the Mondays and Black Grape. What you see is what you get. Plus, it's prime-time Friday-night TV on Channel 4, and people really love *Gogglebox*. Maybe *Celebrity Gogglebox* even more, as people love having a look inside famous people's houses and how they are at home. Although not everyone does it at home, especially when they're doing a one-off for charity or something. You can tell straight away that some of them are in a rented flat or an Airbnb or something because the gaffs they are in just don't look lived in. Me and Bez film it at my house. That's one of the best things about it for me – I don't even have to leave the house! The production crew just come down and set it up. When we were in lockdown during coronavirus, the crew couldn't even come in the house, so they'd just have a production truck parked up outside and have a cable going out of the window. They have some decent celebs on there, too. Robert Plant's been on it, and Martin Kemp is always on there with his kid Ronan, who's a radio DJ, so if it's good enough for Led Zeppelin and Spandau Ballet, it's good enough for me, do you know what I mean?

It's funny the things that people pick up on off *Gogglebox* and find hilarious. There's some things that me or Bez say that we know people will laugh at, like when I said I still think in 'old money' and 'I don't know what metres are, but I know how many grams there are in an ounce.' Obviously I knew what I was saying, or hinting at, and knew that would get a laugh. But then there's other stuff like when I told Bez we were getting 'some of those battery-powered hens' and people thought that was hilarious for some reason. I remember some stuff that Bez has completely forgotten about and, believe it or not, Bez can remember some stuff that I don't have a clue about, and there's some stuff that we both remember but totally differently. People seem to love it, and it's just a bit of fun. It's me and Bez in our sexless marriage. We get to be Bert and Ernie.

# Social media

I think it's best for everyone if I keep my distance from social media, personally. It's just asking for trouble, isn't it? I think people who spend half their life on there are bonkers. They get to thinking that Twitter is real life. It's not. It's full of keyboard warriors saying things they wouldn't have the bottle to in real life, and other people going round and round in circles, tying themselves up in knots. Everyone's got to have an opinion on everything, and they're all getting wound up about things they wouldn't bat an eyelid about in real life.

I've got a Shaun Ryder Twitter account, and one for the Mondays and Black Grape, and we're also on Instagram and Facebook, but I don't look after them myself all the time, which is probably for the best. I do put stuff on there myself occasionally, but I'm not the type to be checking in on social media thirty times a day and posting my opinion about everything and everyone on there. It just seems like an easy way to get yourself into trouble without even leaving the house, you know what I mean? You could just make yourself a brew, sit down, have a look at your phone and, before you know it, get dragged into an argument with some dickhead. Or you put something quite normal up there, and some dick has taken offence at it, reading something into it that you never meant in the first place. From what I can see, there's a lot of keyboard warriors who spend far too much time on there, just looking for an argument. I've seen it happen to so many other musicians and public figures.

See, I'm old school when it comes to those things. I haven't got Siri or Alexa or any of those things that you talk to them and ask them to do things. Predictive texting is bad enough. I'll be trying to text someone about a work thing or something, and the phone will predict something weird like 'I want to see your cock' and suddenly the text has been sent and someone's looking at their phone, thinking 'That's a bit weird, Shaun...' All the kids are sexting now. When I was at school, we had an old-school version of that, which was writing naughty notes on pieces of paper and passing them to girls in class. That was our old-school method of sexting. In fact, because of my dyslexia, I was writing in text-speak years before mobile phones were invented. That was just how I wrote. I struggle with the iPad at home, I've got thumbs that just seem to shut something down or do something mad each time I'm on it, and I have to get my kids to come and sort it.

All these things don't help my ADHD either. As I mentioned before, I've got ADHD and so has Bez, although he won't even go to the doctor, so he's not been diagnosed. At least I'm diagnosed. Bez hasn't got a clue what's wrong with him, although I could tell him a few things. He's definitely got ADHD. You can add that to his list.

Bez told me recently that he even fell out with Siri, after he thought Siri was answering him back. He was trying to use Siri on his phone one day, just talking to it in his normal voice, asking it something, and Siri replied: 'You sound possibly suicidal, would you like to speak to someone? Would you like the number for NHS Direct?' Bez was like, 'What the fuck, Siri? You're supposed to be my mate!'

# Reunions

The Mondays and Black Grape have both reformed and buried our differences. Or most of our differences. The Mondays have been through various reformations, including one with the whole original line-up. We've now got most of the original line-up, apart from our original keyboard player, Paul Davis, and we're better than ever. Kermit and I fell out after the second Black Grape album, but that's all behind us now. Nowadays, I generally do a tour with the Mondays and then one with Black Grape.

Let's face it, most reunions are initially about the cash rather than putting any unfinished business to bed. When we first put the Mondays back together, in 2000, it was pretty much purely a financial decision at first. It wasn't an emotional decision about unfinished business. We were offered the chance to play Manchester Arena, so that was part of the attraction for me because I'd never got to play the Arena as it didn't open until 1995, by which time the

Mondays had long split, and Black Grape never played there. So that was part of the attraction for me. But it was pretty much about the dough.

I don't understand why some bands won't admit that they're getting back together for the cash, when it's clearly obvious. Just be honest. Forget the bullshit excuses about doing it for the love of it, or doing it for the fans, when it's a commercial decision. Bear in mind, bands don't really earn any money from record sales or streaming nowadays. Everyone's got to earn a living. If you're on your arse and someone offers you a big payday to reform the band, then it's hard to turn down. Sure, fans want to come and see you play those songs again, especially if they never saw you first time round, and that's a bonus.

It winds me up a bit if fans get over-protective about '*their* band'. You follow the band, mate, and we appreciate that, but you're not *in* the band. It's not your livelihood. If you lost your job and had no income and were on your arse but then you got offered a sweetener to go back to your old job, I wouldn't begrudge you doing it or put snarky stuff on social media. You might have been lucky enough to see us back in the day, but other people weren't. If you like the band and like the music, why would you begrudge us the chance to make some money out of it? We've got to live and pay the bills and put food on the table just the same as everyone else. If we got back together and no one was interested and we couldn't sell tickets, I'd be fine with that too. If people are no longer interested, then there's not much you can do about it. But if they are, and if I still sell out venues, then I'll go and do it.

When Simon Moran from SJM was putting together the reunion, he knew I wouldn't want to get Mark Day or PD back in the band at that time, so we'd have to find people to replace them. Bez had a few reservations at first, because he was still smarting a bit from the end of the Mondays and how he felt he had been treated at the end of his time in Black Grape. Bez was more concerned than me about the reformed Mondays being seen as a cabaret act, which is a bit ironic. But this was before he'd been in *Big Brother* and everything, and he had his missus and kids to look after, so he couldn't really turn down the money on offer.

There've been various reincarnations of the Mondays since, and in 2015 we got the whole original line-up back together and went on to tour the world. We also did this reality-TV programme called *Singing in the Rainforest*, where we travelled to Panama to record a new song with an isolated tribe called Embera. That was quite a mad trip. Must have been quite mad for the isolated tribe as well, that one of the first people from the Western world they meet is Bez. If they think everyone from the Western world is like Bez they might think they're safer keeping themselves isolated!

Just before we went to Panama to do that show, Paul Davis, the original keyboard player, left again and we replaced him with Dan Broad, and that's been the line-up of the Mondays ever since – the original line-up, plus Rowetta and Dan, and hopefully it will stay that way now.

The Black Grape reunion was easier because it was just me and Kermit, and Bez when's he about. Black Grape was never a set line-up originally really. It was always me and Kermit, plus Bez when he was about, and then a group of session musicians. So, as long as me and Kermit are there, it's Black Grape. To paraphrase Mark E. Smith, if it's me and Kermit and your granny on the bongos, it's Black Grape. We did a reunion tour in 2015 and then went on to make a new album, *Pop Voodoo*, with the legendary producer Youth in 2017, which worked out great. I'd even go as far as saying that *Pop Voodoo* is the proper Black Grape second album, really. *Pop Voodoo* is the album that *Stupid Stupid Stupid* could have been.

Now I've got both bands reunited with the main original members, and they're both sounding great. We're almost better now than we were back in the day, because there's no nonsense. There's less ego involved, as everyone's grown up a bit in that sense, and no hard drugs, as everyone's grown up a lot in that sense. We only do the gigs we want to do, we're not on a relentless tour cycle, and I'm enjoying it more than ever.

# Encore

What would I tell the young Shaun Ryder if I could go back and give him some advice on being a rock star? Dude, there is *nothing* I could tell him. The young Shaun Ryder wouldn't listen to fucking anyone. He didn't listen to his dad, he didn't listen to the rest of the band, he didn't listen to his missus, he didn't listen to Tony Wilson, and he certainly wouldn't listen to me now if I went back and tried to give him some advice. He'd tell me to do one. Looking back now, I thought I knew it all, but I was just a kid really and I had no idea about anything. All the way through the Mondays it was just a free-for-all, a fucking rollercoaster ride where it was every man for himself and no one thought about tomorrow. It was only after the Mondays split that I started to be more aware of how things worked, because I was left on my jack and had to pull Black Grape together and sort a record deal out for the new band. But even then, I was still learning and made a few big mistakes.

What I would like to be able to tell the young me is just to believe in yourself more, make sure you enjoy it more, and you don't need a shedload of drugs to do it, mate. Or not quite so many anyway. I really do wish I had enjoyed it more than I did. But it was relentless. What can you do apart from just ride it? Rock'n'roll doesn't come with a guidebook. It's such a weird fucking existence that nothing can fully prepare you for it, no matter how many documentaries or books you've read about your favourite bands. You've just got to ride it, which we did. I'd just tell the younger me: 'Fucking hell, mate, just lighten up a bit!'

Same for the rest of the Mondays – I'd just tell them to believe in themselves more, because none of us really believed in ourselves back then. We were always doubting ourselves. I never owned any of our records for years, didn't even have a copy in the house. Then, when they were rereleasing the first couple of albums a few years ago, I got sent copies of them and listened to them for the first time in about twenty years, and I thought, 'This is great, this is really good.' I wish we'd appreciated what we were doing a bit more at the time instead of just picking holes in it and pushing ourselves, thinking 'We can do better than this, come on, we can do better.'

Once I knew that we'd been given a chance to be in this world – in this game, the music business or the entertainment business or whatever you want to call it – I wasn't throwing it away. I really wasn't. I knew from day one that I didn't want to throw it away, that this was my chance. Once we'd got on *Top of the Pops* and 'made it', I was determined not to throw it away. I knew how privileged we were to get a break, and I'm not sure the rest of the Mondays did when they first split the band. I can always remember them saying, 'I'd rather be on the dole than work with Shaun Ryder.' Really? Well, be careful what you wish for, because that's what happened to them.

Always remember rock'n'roll is a game. Don't forgot that. Don't take yourself too fucking seriously. Mick Jagger had it right: 'I know, it's only rock'n'roll, but I like it.' I never thought I'd last this long in the game, and I think it's my greatest achievement, but now I'm here I don't want to retire. What else am I going to do? My missus Joanne wouldn't let me retire anyway. She wouldn't want me round the house, under her feet all day. I'm going to keep doing this until I'm dead.

Would I try and put off my younger kids if they wanted to go into music? No, absolutely not, because they're arty types. That's how they've been brought up and what they're interested in, so I don't think you should ever deny that. It's what's inside them, isn't it? I believe that we're all pretty much pre-programmed. No matter how much I tried, I could never be an electrician or a carpenter. I could spend eight hours a day training to be a carpenter, but I'd never be any good at it because my brain is not wired that way. People who are natural carpenters, it just makes sense to them. They get a piece of wood in their hands, and it just feels natural. If you're wired inside to be a carpenter or an electrician or a politician, then you're not programmed inside to make music or write books. My kids are wired to have an artistic side, so they'll probably end up doing something artistic or related to that, and hopefully they'll find something they're happy doing which satisfies that.

It's like back when we were kids – we were into music, and we found the best way for us to express that was to start our own band and make our own music. When acid house kicked off it changed people's lives and people thought differently about what they could do. Some people decided they wanted to try and make music and be a DJ, but some people weren't wired that way inside, so maybe they started to design record covers or flyers for club nights and then ended up a graphic designer, or maybe they ended up a lighting designer or building stages or something. I believe that everyone is wired differently inside, and if you're lucky you find something that you're into, that you're actually pretty good at. It turned out that I was pretty good at making up rhymes and little bits that came together as songs, but I wasn't wired inside like some other front men are. I wasn't wired inside to be that cliché version of a rock star, who is prancing around at the front of the stage, lapping up the attention... so I had to find my own slightly different way of being a rock star. Which I did, and I think that's what helped us last so long, and why we're still here forty years later – the fact that we were original and different. You could probably say about all of the Mondays, and Kermit from Black Grape, that they were all wired pretty differently – Bez certainly fucking was – and that's what made us unique. We didn't look like anyone else. We didn't think like anybody else. We didn't act like anyone else. We were out there on our own trip. We approached music in a different way to anyone else and didn't sound like anyone else. Sometimes you need a bit of distance to see how true that is.

I'm enjoying life more and more. More than I ever did. I'm more comfortable with myself and more confident in myself. I know who I am and what I'm capable of. I'm really looking forward to making the next record, I'm looking forward to new TV projects. As long as I like doing it, and I'm enjoying it, then that's great.

I never wanted to live fast and die young. Live fast, yes. Die young, no. Fuck that. I might have been on a bit of a self-destruct path for a while, but I never had a death wish. There's too much to live for. I always wanted to stick around, and I'm happier than I've ever been now, and more at peace with myself. I'm too old to die young and leave a beautiful corpse now, anyway. It's a bit too late for that, mate.